ARTURO B. FALLICO was born, and received his early education, in Italy. He received his Ph.D. in philosophy at Northwestern University, where he also taught. He presently teaches philosophy at San Jose State College in California. He was honored in 1955 with a Ford Foundation Award to study the role of philosophy in general education. His Knoles Lectures at the University of the Pacific were published as *The Quest for Authentic Existence*. Many other articles have appeared in scholarly journals here and abroad. In addition to having studied with Benedetto Croce, Professor Fallico is himself a painter and sculptor, and a teacher of these arts.

ART &
EXISTENTIALISM

Arturo B. Fallico

PRENTICE-HALL, INC.
Englewood Cliffs, N.J.

To the memory of
my mother

Preface

What important existentialist literature there is on the subject of aesthetics is, for the most part, scattered in journals not readily available. Little of it, moreover, is in the English language, largely because of the wide and fundamental difference between European and Anglo-American philosophical concerns during the first half of the twentieth century.

Present attempts at an existentialist aesthetic reflect diversities and likenesses similar to those of the major existentialist ontologies. The distinctive view of existing individual man and his freedom, the element of self-disclosure in crisis and decision, the matter of ultimate concern, the view of the world as concrete life-world (*Lebenswelt*)—each plays its role. Despite the common threads, however, it remains difficult to relate what is explicitly said or implied by writers like Sartre, Heidegger, Marcel, and Camus on the aesthetic problem. On the whole, existentialist-phenomenological philosophy remains vitally individualistic; perhaps an unavoidable condition of this manner of philosophizing. Perhaps it is too early to draw up any account of its achievements.

But that the ontological question, as to the *meaning of Being,* is at the heart of existentialist thought, there can be no doubt. This is no longer a question of the traditional metaphysics, but a more interiorized version. The question is now asked: Who but some particular being, who but existing man himself, can ask the question about Being? And does not such a question, therefore, address itself first and foremost to the being of the existent who asks it? Thus the first question of philosophy is Sören Kierkegaard's anguished *What does it mean to exist?*

In existential terms, the question of art remains intrinsically tied to an ontology of existence and of being generally. The basic form of the question is: How must a being be constituted, in his very being, so that art can be possible? Admittedly, such a question is enough to overwhelm and discourage any inquirer. But philosophy itself, in the existentialist tradition, is at bottom nothing but a kind of courage.

As far as I know, this is the first attempt at a comprehensive existentialist aesthetics. It therefore raises more questions than it poses directly and tries to answer, but none, it is hoped, that cannot be formulated and answered in the terms and context put forth. It may be assumed that, not only in existentialist, but in all other kinds of philosophy as well, what makes any question pertinent and meaningful is its respect for the terms and context of thinking whence it springs, and to which it is addressed.

I have tried to avoid technical jargon, keeping in mind the average intelligent reader. One difficulty, inherent in a work of this sort, could not be eliminated. This is what might be called "the difficulty of saying the obvious." It is a strange and remarkable fact about professional philosophers and their readers, that specialistic vocabularies which often refer to nothing that can be experienced acquire "meaning," whereas the concrete, and the language of the concrete, seem recondite and even meaningless. Serious description of the concrete and the obvious such as we are attempting here, calls for a clearing of the eyes, so to speak, and a restoration of language to its vital and original expressive uses: both of these operations are difficult in an age when useful abstractions have become more real and more significant than the plain concrete realities displayed before our eyes.

The ordering of the parts of this book presented the writer with some problems. The general reader might read the middle part, "Art and Existence," before the rest, in order to enter directly and comprehensively into the subject. For the systematic student of existentialist thought, however, it seemed advisable to prepare the ground with a more gradual approach. In any case, the book as a whole was planned to reflect something of the organic nature of the subject discussed; significant themes are often first introduced in embryonic form and more fully articulated later. Repetition is deliberate and in ever-widening contexts. Here and there in the footnotes the reader is reminded of this.

The list of my intellectual benefactors is long—from Plato to Sartre, in fact. Though cast in the mold of my own thinking, insights of Benedetto Croce, and Jean-Paul Sartre, among others, are in evidence on nearly every page. My grateful acknowledgment goes also to my friends and colleagues, Professors William Brandt and Fredrik Feltham: the first for his invaluable help in reading portions of the manuscript, and the second for a life-long exchange of ideas on art and life. To my old student and faithful friend, Mrs. Luisa Baldanzi, I remain grateful for typing and editing considerable portions of this work. To Myrtle Dean Clark I owe the encouragement and help which have made my intellectual efforts possible. My thanks go also to the University of the Pacific Publications in Philosophy and its chief editor, William D. Nietmann, for permission to use parts of my Knoles Lectures.

A. B. F.

Table of Contents

xi

ART &

EXISTENTIALISM

CHAPTER ONE

Philosophy & Existence

PHENOMENOLOGY AND EXISTENTIALISM

Although existential phenomenology[1] has been one of the dominant philosophical movements on the European continent for well over a quarter century, it may seem to the American student—brought up in a different tradition—perversely paradoxical. Is not existentialism a subjective view of life and the world, and phenomenology a quasi-scientific philosophical concern? As a matter of fact, they are complementary.

Existentialism is a fundamental position from which to view human experience. Modern phenomenology, on the other hand, is primarily a method of analysis. Hence existential phenomenology transcends its components, and is a true and complete philosophy. On this ground, one may reasonably examine it to see what its im-

---

[1] For a comprehensive history of Phenomenology see Herbert Spiegelberg, *The Phenomenological Movement* (The Hague, Netherlands: Martinus Nijhoff, 1960). Sources for Existentialism are generally of two kinds: literary, and philosophical. Most of the plays and novels of Jean-Paul Sartre and Albert Camus are available in English translation. The best philosophical sources remain the major works of Martin Heidegger and Jean-Paul Sartre. Major works are Sartre's *L'Être et le néant*; and Heidegger's *Sein und Zeit*. The works of earlier influential writers are all available in excellent translations; the student's attention is called especially to those of Sören Kierkegaard, Blaise Pascal, and Friedrich Nietzsche. Other recommended available sources: Gabriel Marcel, *The Mystery of Being* (Chicago: Henry Regnery Co., 1960); Paul Tillich, *The Courage to Be* (New Haven: Yale University Press, 1952).

1

plications are for any area of philosophic concern. Just as there is a
Thomistic aesthetic, even though St. Thomas never composed a
treatise on aesthetics, there is an aesthetic implicit in existential
phenomenology. That is the subject of this study.

A natural alliance was inherent in existentialism and phenomenology from their inceptions because both were formulated as
assaults upon the dominance of idealism and positivism, in one
form or another, in nineteenth century Europe. The relationship
of phenomenology to idealism and positivism is clear; phenomenology represents one facet of the original enemy of both. It represents, as a matter of fact, a revival of the logical and ontological
opposition to the extremes in Medieval nominalism and realism.
The long and varied history of the special sensitivity now called
existentialism is not easy to trace. But it is clear enough that the
modern form of this affective posture, as represented by such diverse
thinkers as Sören Kierkegaard, Friedrich Nietzsche, and the young
Karl Marx,[2] manifests rebellion against the newer forms of idealism
and positivism as one of its basic themes.

The phenomenology associated with contemporary existentialism
first took shape in the work of Franz Brentano (1838-1917), Alexius
Meinong (1853-1920), and Edmund Husserl (1859-1938). It began
with a theory of mind derived, as some believe, from the Scholastic
notion of "intentionality." According to this theory, mind or consciousness, by its very nature, "intends" the object—refers to something beyond itself; it is always consciousness *of* something. It is as
if, in becoming aware of anything, the mind reaches out for objects
whose very character as objects remains tied and bound to the
mind's act of appropriation. Hence, the primary fact about consciousness is its consciousness of *things*. On this basis, Alexius
Meinong called his philosophy a "theory of objects." However,
notwithstanding the tentacle-like hold of consciousness on objects,
the objects themselves remain independent and identifiable. In
Meinong's view, such objects include Platonic ideas, mathematical
entities, immediately perceived qualities of sense, logical propositions, and even self-contradictions such as "round squares." All
things that could be thought about were, in his view, equally independent of being thought about.

For Husserl, to study consciousness was to study mind in the act

[2] A. B. Fallico, *The Quest for Authentic Existence* (Stockton, California: College of the Pacific Publications in Philosophy, 1958), pp. 71-72.

of grasping some object beyond itself and incorporating it. He took phenomenological description to be a description of consciousness-of-objects. He therefore could not but raise the question of how this consciousness-of-objects could be observed and analyzed. For if consciousness is awareness of objects, how can any consciousness be left over, so to speak, to carry on investigation of awareness itself? Passing over certain intricacies in his thinking on this point, it is sufficient to say that Husserl found the solution to this problem in the intrinsically *reflexive* character of consciousness itself—consciousness can be aware of itself as a consciousness-of-object. In this self-reflective capacity of mind, he saw the possibility for an act of radical disengagement that could free consciousness from itself *qua* consciousness-of-objects, achieving a dual vision by which it both worked, and could observe itself doing so. The mind could therefore achieve a vantage point from which to observe itself from the outside, as it were, as a consciousness whose very nature it is to be in touch with objects. Phenomenology has investigated the character of that contact. This it could do in a perfectly detached or objective way, since by temporarily withdrawing the inner activity of consciousness from the subject-object relation it stands back from its own activity so that it can attend to that relation. Ordinarily when consciousness is simply involved in and with the subject-object relation it does not have this relation *before* itself as object to survey or examine.

Cartesian and British empiricists had conceived of immediate, pre-reflective, or pre-conceptualized experience as a collection of private and atomic sense data or impressions. The early phenomenologists tried to show that such a view was artificial. They thought of pre-reflective experience as a system of intentions opening into a world, a world belonging to Man's very being prior to scientific and philosophical conceptualizations. They noted the obvious fact that, before we begin to reflect about it, we are already in, and involved with, the world; and after we have reflected, we find ourselves still in it. To see the ever-present and pervasive realm of the concrete, the pre-reflective, and to be able properly to inspect, describe and analyze its structures, a special method was called for. This method would make it possible to hold the intentional object of consciousness steady and in focus before an inspecting consciousness freed from all scientific and metaphysical preconceptions, to say nothing of vagrant remnants of "common-sense" experience.

As a result of such laying bare of intending consciousness, there was posited a *being-in-the-world* which stands prior to all subjective and objective being, and which represents the source of this distinction. This source is the *life-world* (*Lebenswelt*), in and with which existing man has his existential being. The subsequent exploration cut through both idealistic and positivistic perspectives, disclosing a primordial realm of being from which all reflective enterprises must feed, and to which they all must return their produce. This basic life-world structure incorporates all perspectives in a pattern called *in-der-Welt-Sein* by Martin Heidegger, and *l'être au monde* by Sartre and Merleau-Ponty. Existing man is seen as a moving system of intentions which pervade the things and agencies with which he must unavoidably live and have his being, and which give those things meaning.[3] Nonetheless, the things and agencies have autonomous being and meaning, because this is what consciousness intends for them. The life-world is thus indissolubly bound up with the existent whose world it is, but must be discovered as something on its own; that is, as phenomenologically discoverable as independent of both subjective and objective. The existent must somehow extricate himself from this world inseparable from his intentions, so as to know it, but must do so without breaking his bond with it or reducing it to something that is not *for* him. In this way phenomenology focuses on the concrete—on the object caught in the richest possible nexus of relationships: our "focal" and our "peripheral" vision of it combine into a single act. The battle cry of phenomenology has been "Let us get back to *things!*"

Brentano and Meinong conceived of phenomenology as a complete philosophy, not just a method. Modern existentialism, beginning with Heidegger, has used it as a method. More accurately, existentialism has found in phenomenology a methodology which can make systematizations possible, for phenomenology has unflaggingly directed its attention in a deliberate and conscious way to what existentialism had been groping for in an unsystematic way: the point of dynamic intersection between consciousness and its world. Phenomenology provided existentialism, moreover, with a perspective that yields evidence available to all. One need but accept the testimony of one's own consciousness, which is, after all, the only witness an individual has to his own existence. If the human consciousness can offer any valid evidence at all, modern

[3] John Wild, ed., "Man and His Life-World," in *Nine Essays in Phenomenology, For Roman Ingarden* (The Hague, Netherlands: Martinus Nijhoff, 1959).

phenomenology offers a true[4] perspective for philosophizing about human experience.

We mentioned earlier that the genealogy of the existentialist motif is not easy to trace. Much of its modern impulse derives from Sören Kierkegaard's moody reflections on the state of nineteenth century Christianity, and his attack upon Hegel's system armed with an adaptation of Hegel's own weapons. Nietzsche's cry that "God is dead, and what shall we do about it" played no small part. The influence of Karl Marx—the "last of the Scholastics," as he has been called, especially of his early works—was clearly to make a moral issue of the dejected state of nineteenth century existing man, decrying the fact that man had been reduced to the status of a mere product for sale to the highest bidder. Blaise Pascal's central theme of man's fallen estate and fearful condition of being gains even him a place in this tradition. Existentialism represents a strand of thought present in every age and among all peoples; the persistent sensitivity, the fundamental mood, the disturbing awareness which it represents, is stamped on every product of the human spirit that attests man's radical ontological insecurity, born out of the deepest self-consciousness.

This is the tradition of existing man's concern with his individual self—with his own soul. He has forever reflected upon the irremediable contingency of his being, his mortality, his forlornness, his solitariness, his uncertain fate. Under the sway of this mood, existing man has time and again become aware of his unessentiality of being, his essence-lessness, as if awakening naked and homeless in a Parmenidean universe of immobile Essence. This, surely, is the state of awareness which has ever instilled in existing man the feeling of being a stranger, a wanderer without abode or destination, or a prisoner awaiting release or execution for some original, forgotten crime. Beginning at least with St. Augustine, this tradition, too, is one in which the subjective core-reality of the existing being has awakened to its desperate sense of freedom and personal responsibility in the face of death and nothingness. Moreover, the freedom thus self-disclosed is something quite different from that freedom of choice so heatedly disputed by the academic philosophers. It is a freedom in which the will exercises itself independently of any determinant whatsoever, be it instinct or impulse, passion, rational or moral motives, character, or the "self." It has no other cause than the spontaneous power to decide and will, whose choices and vo-

[4] For the definition of "true," as used in the text, see p. 165.

litions are explicable simply and solely by its mere existence and exercise, and require no other reason of any sort to account for them. Freedom and *spontaneity* are here synonymous.[5]

An inquiring mind seems always to cast its eyes first on the things farthest removed from existing man. Only later does it take notice of existing man himself as a unique being who, in a special sense, can be said to be the only being that really *is there,* since he alone knows himself to be there. In this way he discovers himself to be the only being who *exists,* as Heidegger says.[6] Other things merely *are;* they do not exist. Hence, man always returns from excursions into knowledge rich in "knowledge about" but poor in "understanding of." He does not understand the things he thought he knew, and thus becomes the most pressing problem to himself. Like Socrates, he turns his eyes away from things "on the other side of the moon," seeking avidly for self-knowledge instead.

But as soon as the quest after self-knowledge starts it discloses the profound schism between existing man's unique kind of being and all that is other. Upon this realization there follows another: though a deep gulf divides man from his non-human world, the break is neither radical nor "given"; it is more in the nature of a polarity than a duality. After the ratiocinative mind has done its worst to deepen the gulf, the mind's primordial union with its world at its very foundations remains patent and undisturbed. Consciousness and the world which it intends arise together. Nevertheless, before the pre-reflective life-world is unearthed from the heap of the mind's own constructions and fabrications, subjectivity itself may be declared to be supernatural in origin, nature, and destiny, though somehow bound to a world whose time and being are fast running out. Under other and more favorable circumstances, subjectivity may be taken as a real pole in tension with what is "other," irreducible to that other and vice versa. The man who realizes his true condition as an existing being never is willing to resolve his inner self into the realm of mere things thereby reducing himself to a function, a body, or an insensate process. Nevertheless, an interiorized view of existence-in-the-world and of the life-world is reached which differs fundamentally from anything found in science or in speculative philosophy.

[5] Although tied to theological and other interests, the interminable argument on this subject, beginning especially with the 12th century, served to keep alive the problem of human freedom now being re-examined by existentialist thinkers.

[6] This is an important aspect of the meaning of *Dasein* in Heidegger's *Sein und Zeit.*

Phenomenology and existentialism both inherently seek to go beyond or underneath the abstracting mind and all its intellectual edifices, bent on restoring a presupposition-less standpoint from which immediate concrete experience can be directly confronted and examined. Both search for a way of extricating the active consciousness from tendentious involvements, freeing it to see what is there to be seen, and to see itself at the same time. Such involvements are *non-cognitive* expressions of the free act; they represent only its release, not its self-possessed exercise. In short, both phenomenology and existentialism aim at bringing the concrete life-world into clear view.

The introduction of phenomenological method into existentialist concerns has meant a transition from unsystematic and literary expressions, such as Nietzsche's *Zarathustra,* to technical writings such as Heidegger's *Sein und Zeit* and Sartre's *L'Être et le néant.* For phenomenology, on the other hand, the existentialist assimilation has meant an equally significant change in application to problems of concrete human existence instead of the "essences" with which it was previously concerned. It is remarkable that a passionate and even personal kind of interrogation could join a dispassionate and almost mathematical method of inquiry, to the reciprocal gain of both.

For writers such as Heidegger, this historical joining of efforts marks the re-discovery of the original purpose and intent of philosophizing itself. For others, it marks at least the rejoining of philosophical with ontologico-religious and aesthetic interests which seemed long ago to have been lost in the sterile dehumanization of Western philosophy, which tended to make of philosophy either a handmaiden to the sciences of nature or a sub-division of the literary arts.

I find myself in agreement with certain of these appraisals. For example, it seems to me that phenomenological method alone is finally inadequate to deal with the existentialist's fundamental question: what is the meaning of Being? But insofar as the method effectively helps us to explore the life-world and its phenomena, this study attests to the author's acceptance of it.[7]

[7] While not transcending the concreteness of human experience, the quest for the meaning of being in any final sense would involve, I believe, so much further "interiorizing" of the depth-philosophy which is Existentialism that it might be more suitable to call it by some other name; "existential religion," perhaps.

PHILOSOPHY AND THE EXISTING INDIVIDUAL

In the existentialist-phenomenological view, philosophy has to do with the discovery of what really is before us in that which we accept as commonplace, ordinary, and "obvious." It neither speculates beyond what appears, nor rearranges what appears in order to make things more amenable to observation. It searches for no hidden realities. Thus, philosophy is necessarily difficult. For, contrary to what is commonly supposed, that which stands simply and plainly exhibited before our very eyes is not easy truly to understand. Layer upon layer of culturally derived preconceptions and predispositions obscure a direct view of life and of the life-world. Philosophy is difficult just because it requires us to be simple: to look at what is there to be seen, see it, and describe it. It asks us neither to construct something nor to add something to that which we confront within and outside ourselves. Of this we shall make it a point to remind the reader at every turn.

The philosophical effort consists of two distinct phases or moments. The first involves a radical clearing away of all that obstructs direct vision; the second, an exercise of the unobstructed vision thus obtained. In its first phase, the philosophical effort moves to find and to gain a fresh perspective, free of all conceptual products and elaborations, so that the intended object of consciousness can be brought into critical focus. In its second phase, it inspects that object with discrimination. But—and this is the distinctive feature of existentialist philosophizing—*the object scrutinized remains bound by his intentionality to the observer.* For this reason, inspection of the object must lead back to the intending observer whose thought about it defines the object he is observing. It necessarily follows that the description of an object must disclose something about the subject, even something of his very condition of being. In this important respect, an existentialist aesthetic is part and parcel of an ontology of existence, as well as ontology in general.[8]

Philosophy as an activity—philosophy of art, for example—is not simply the production of a painting or engagement in an act of

---

[8] See Chapter Four.

art appreciation. We must philosophize—learn to do philosophy. How do we go about finding out how to do this?

Philosophical "knowledge" is frequently negatively depicted, as being neither scientific knowledge nor poetic realization. It is sometimes claimed that philosophical knowledge is not really the article presumedly delivered by the traditional philosophies. However that may be, we may feel inclined to take the common suggestion to acquaint ourselves with the work of those reputed to have philosophized successfully. We read books, consider the kinds of questions that are asked, follow the arguments that are put forth, and take note of the conclusions reached. We observe the different ways in which philosophers put the same question and how some question may be a crucial one to some philosophers but entirely irrelevant in the view of others.[9]

But what if we are unable to find by this method a common thread binding philosophical undertakings together? Viewed with their intentions in mind, philosophies and philosophers differ as much as Aristotle differs from Hume, or the mystic Jacob Boehme from the positivist Carnap. In fact, few experts agree that philosophy is a single-minded undertaking. Bertrand Russell thinks that the whole tradition initiated by Socrates was a regrettable mistake.[10] Benedetto Croce held that nearly all that goes under the name of philosophy is in the nature of a support to theological interests entirely extraneous to philosophy as he understood it. Wittgenstein seems to hold that the whole of the philosophical venture is a sort of mental aberration resulting from misuse of language. Marx and his followers view other philosophers as dupes of capitalist usurpers.

In the course of this inevitable, discouraging recognition, we may fancy we see a ray of hope. Some philosophers, in addition to building philosophies and justifying them, also have endeavored to say what philosophizing *itself* is, or should be—they philosophize about philosophizing. Such effort has been persistent enough to permit us to speak of a history of "the philosophy of philosophy." [11]

[9] Contemporary existentialist ontologies represent, generally, an attempt to come to a metaphysics founded on a radical empirical psychology.

[10] Bertrand Russell, *A History of Western Philosophy* (New York: Simon and Schuster, 1945). Especially chapters on Socrates, Plato, and the Scholastics.

[11] The expression is Hegel's, in line with his view that philosophy is the Self-consciousness of the Idea. In a different sense, any thinker who has given attention to the nature of the philosophical endeavor can be said to have concerned himself with the philosophy of philosophy.

Surely this is a valid discovery, for here the philosophers not only
build their systems, but account for what they are doing. To judge
from such accounts, the act of philosophizing is a struggling for
self-conscious self-possession, delivering a form of self-certifying,
self-identifying, purposive activity which should, when directed
upon any form of human experience, authoritatively certificate and
help identify it, too.

But alas, such efforts turn out to be little more than an extension
of philosophical system-spinning. They faithfully reflect no more
than what the philosophers did in building their systems. The self-
accountings turn out to be supports for the systems. But is this not
to be expected? A philosopher might as well do what everyone else
does when he tries to account for what he is doing or has committed himself to do. We all account for our doings in terms of
the purposes we have espoused and the means we have preferred
to carry them out. How would it strike us if a shoemaker, say, intent on making shoes, should account for what he is doing, by saying that "to make shoes is to plow a field"? Self-accounting must be
redundant: the question, "What am I doing?" normally not only
coalesces with the question, "What should I be doing?" but the
answer is the answer to the questions, "What do I want to do?"
and, "How is what I want to do best done?" The accounts of what
we are up to when we are philosophizing (or doing anything else,
for that matter) must be *ex post facto*.

A shoemaker's accounting of his activity, if it is a thoughtful
accounting, carries no compulsion that everybody else engage in the
making of shoes. Accounts given by philosophers carry no particular
injunction that we espouse their causes, either. To be sure, those
secretly longing to become shoemakers, Platonists, Spencerians,
Wittgensteinians, or whatever, are always with us, and to them the
accounts of their idols will carry a certain persuasive force which
will be interpreted as compelling encounters with Truth. Perhaps
none of us is immune to such suggestions if a subjective "set," as
psychologists call latent predisposition, is in our bosoms waiting to
throb. We may find it easy to resist some ways of philosophizing,
but not all; some way can always be found which matches our needs
or jibes with our secret hopes, resentments, weaknesses, or fancied
roles. For, existentially speaking, behind every philosophy and every
account of philosophizing there stands something that somebody
somewhere, sometime, has come to prize. The two—the philosophy
and would-be philosopher—need only meet and a sort of copulation

occurs, which produces issue. Even though such unions occur philosophizing carries no really compelling force other than that surreptitious but pretentious one generated by the word "Truth" when backed by professorial pose, institutional authority, or personal reputation. None of those supports really imparts value to what is professed. Even if no one else is successfully deceiving us we can always deceive ourselves.

It is true that what is called logic, together with logic's inseparable twin, the *system,* is often brought to bear upon the article offered as a kind of sure and confident persuader, or proof that one should join the crowd or be ashamed of himself for not doing so. But the necessitation in any system is internal to the system, enclosed within its own frame of reference. Systems themselves are never necessitated by their own internal rules and demands. One is ruled by both general and specific ways of moving within the system only after one chooses to submit to them, not before. Inviting an existing man to enter a system is like inviting him to play a game of chess. If he refuses, he cannot be forced to play by the rules of the game itself. The most effective means of getting people to agree to be rational are usually non-rational, even irrational.

A certain Western philosopher, attending an East-West conference of philosophers at the University of Hawaii some years back, after listening attentively to a paper read by an important Chinese philosopher, said to him: "But, don't you see that you have contradicted yourself?" "Of course I do!" the Chinese philosopher replied. "In China we have been successful in doing this for many centuries!"

The question we must now ask is whether we are constitutionally so caught up in our activities that the *what* and *why* of our activities can refer only to the chosen thing we are after, and to the ways of getting it. We must ask if there is not some other possibility of accounting for what we do, no matter what we do, than to say that we do what we are doing because we must. If there is no other possibility, it must then be admitted that all our activities, including philosophizing, are and forever must remain self-unaccounting.[12] There would then be no point in looking for answers to such questions as "What is art?" "What is science?" What is

---

[12] That philosophical or religious concerns can be the subject of psychological analysis of one kind or another seems by many to be resented as degrading these interests; to the existentialist, philosophy is itself a form of psychoanalysis in the Delphic sense—*Gnosci te ipsum.*

philosophy?" Such questions could be answered only by performing those activities for oneself. Under such a limitation, what could the questioner possibly wish to know about art, science, or philosophy that would not be clear to him if he took the trouble to learn about them, and acquire the ability to do these things? The limitation suggests purposeful self-inspection of purposing activity levels, each inspecting another underlying it—an infinite regress. In this light the traditional indifference, even contempt, that creative producers of art and science have sometimes shown for the philosopher's prattle about their work is perhaps justified.[13]

The agent of all our concrete activities is their *do-er*, the *act-or* —the existing individual man. Under certain conditions of his existence, this subject-agent does in fact ask about the what and the why of things, including his own activity in asking the question, in a way that unmistakably indicates the possibility and presence of a *free* vantage point for inquiry. An existing man is not simply a collection of functions or a biological urge.[14] The fundamental problem in our quest after philosophy is to locate not an act, but a kind of man. Fichte said that the philosophy a man professes depends on the kind of man he is. Significantly, Fichte had in mind the abysmal difference between the kind of man who chooses to be his own freedom, and the kind who chooses to merge instead with any unfreedom that the ratiocinative mind can concoct. With the discovery of the man who can come to the self-disclosure of what it means to exist, our journey of exploration begins. We started by asking a question, hoping that we could find the answer in the philosophical endeavor; we arrive instead, not at any answer, but at the questioner himself. For questions are asked only by existing men. Except for a living man of flesh and bone, not a question would be heard in the boundless ocean of being in which we are cast. Galaxies could thunder through the heavens, Sputniks unwind their pre-arranged beeps, but otherwise all would be silence, except as man, or some being like a man, could speak to ask a question. Except for an existing man, everything remains unnamed, unaccounted for, and self-unaccounting. In the universe only human voices are heard even though they report the hearing of superhuman voices.[15]

[13] See also p. 156.
[14] A. B. Fallico "Existentialism and Education," *J. Ed. Theory*, Vol. IV, No. 2 (April 1954).
[15] A. B. Fallico, *The Quest for Authentic Existence*, p. 9.

The existential man we are discussing is not all of man. There are many ways of completing the sentence, "Yes, but man is also . . . ." But the existential view of man must be acknowledged by all thoughtful and perceptive men, no matter how they propose to complete such a sentence. For our present purposes, the existential man is sufficient. This doer, this subject-agent, is usually immersed in his projects, with only that degree of awareness of his condition necessary to effect his purposes, whatever they may be. Yet he is also manifestly capable of an existential state in which, as a purposer, he is stripped of his purposes, and thus capable of a unique kind of objectivity. Let me propose three examples of this condition—expressed both seriously and jestfully—one of which I shall comment upon at length.

It is reported that at the close of his philosophical career, when he had ceased writing philosophy, St. Thomas Aquinas remarked quite seriously: "All that I have done now appears to me as straw."

On the occasion of being presented with an official union card by the Plumber's Union, Albert Einstein was reported to have remarked: "I wish now that I had been a plumber instead of a physicist."

Whether they are serious or in jest (jest has its own serious side; Einstein spoke at a time when he and everyone else was asking whether science was not about to destroy mankind itself) we cannot presume to reconstruct all that was intended by these remarks, but it seems reasonable to suppose that Aquinas and Einstein were giving evidence of being able to disengage themselves from their special interests enough to question them as a whole, and to speak as men concerned with a much wider scope and view of human existence and its problems. They were no longer *in* their special undertakings, but out, free of the peculiar demands that these make, looking upon and appraising them in the light of man's total condition, and of much more. By such remarks, men might very well have been disowned, ostracized by their respective scholarly associations. But each showed his essential humanity, his ability to see and to acknowledge truths beyond those that reason or scientific preoccupations can deliver. It takes a great mind to give birth to the *Summa*, or the formula $E = mc^2$, but it takes a full man, aware of himself as an existing person having a relation to other persons and to the world as a whole, to speak honestly, and as if capable of annulling such accomplishments, if needs be, in view of the larger problem of man himself and his predicament.

I once asked a butcher why he was doing what he did, anticipating nothing more than some simple account of how he came to be a butcher. Surprisingly, the butcher replied: "To tell you the truth, Mister, I really don't know why I am doing this or anything else." Further conversation disclosed that in answering the question in this way, the butcher had none of the following motives in mind:

"I shouldn't have gotten into this business in the first place, there's no money in it," or

"I wish I could get into some other work that is more satisfying," or

"I can't take this chopping up animals any longer," or

"I don't know what psychological compulsion makes me want to butcher," or

"I had an argument with the boss and feel like quitting." What the man had in mind was, rather, something like this: "To tell you the truth, Mister, I really don't know why I am doing this or anything else. As a matter of fact, I don't even know who I am, or what I am supposed to be and to do, even though everybody else seems to know the moment I pull out my Social Security card or my driver's license. Even to repeat my name to myself, or to remember where I live, and with whom, doesn't seem to help. The bottom of my world has dropped out, and with it, the very meaning of my existence. I can't quite tell you how this mess came about, since nothing spectacular or momentous has ever happened to me. Maybe I'm just bored. The remarkable thing is that although everything, including myself, has lost all meaning I still find myself feeling, thinking, and asking questions about it all."

The man had stopped espousing any and all special projects. Had he been a philosopher or a scientist, he might have said the same thing. His values had collapsed *in toto*. He had pulled out from under all his doings; disconsolate, to be sure, but in possession of a perspective from which he could question everything as if he were the creator of it all, who, disillusioned, had no use for his own creation. Exclusive attention to the particular purposes and valued ends for which he previously acted could no longer constitute rock-bottom base for self-accounting, or accounting for any of his projects. All that was left with him was the bare act of the purposer, the dis-attached but supremely self-conscious spontaneity of being apart from all that he formerly attached to his being by way of deciding and valuing. In the wreck, he himself, to be sure, was also submerged, but still present and in full possession of himself. He could observe the ruins and give exact account of his condition. In a way, he had become more clearly aware of what it meant for him to exist than many another man, lost and submerged in unself-conscious projectings, in a state in which impersonality of action and thought creates the illusion that everything that one does or thinks is self-evidently and intrinsically valuable and meaningful to his existence. The butcher was in existential distress, but no one could accuse him of being lost in the smog of what Heidegger calls *"das Mann,"*—the man of unauthentic existence—who becomes in his own estimate a "we," a "they," or an "it."

What occasioned the butcher to disengage himself from all the petty and grave concerns of life is the disengagement disclosed to him by his own existential condition. If it be objected that such disengagement of the doer from his activities involves a critical condition of existence—of interest, perhaps, only to the psychiatrist, and hence of no real value as basis for philosophical inquiry—it may be noted that it is at least questionable whether many of those states of being which have hitherto been regarded as pathological are not rather fundamentally existential, natural and unavoidable culminations or crises in living, marking the point where genuine decisions stand to be made. Certainly some of the most promising work in phenomenological psychiatry has been undertaken on the premise that some sort of existential perception underlies much that is considered psychological pathology.[16] Martin Heidegger has shown that boredom, despair, and confrontation of mortality are effective in opening one's eyes to the startling fact of existence as well as to authentic living. Both Gabriel Marcel, the Catholic existentialist, and Albert Camus, an agnostic, if not an atheist, suggest that fundamental thinking about life and the world begins with the realization that suicide is always possible for any man. Camus even holds that authentic existence is possible only as we squarely face and accept the total absurdity of life and the world, determining to make our humanity count in spite of, and against it.[17]

[16] Existentialist psychoanalysis, also sometimes referred to as Logotherapy, has long been developing on the European mainland. Maurice Merleau-Ponty is chief exponent of this view; his *Phénoménologie de la perception* (Paris: Bibliothèque des idées, 1948) is especially recommended; in the U.S. Rollo May and others are doing much to make existentialist psychoanalysis known.

[17] Gabriel Marcel, *The Philosophy of Existence* (New York: Philosophical Library, 1949), p. 14; Albert Camus, *The Myth of Sisyphus and other Essays* (New York: Alfred A. Knopf, 1955).

To me, there seems to be no special reason for supposing that a free inquiry can emerge only from the terrifying and gloomy crises that existentialists, for the most part, dwell upon. The existential situations and vicissitudes of life are many, and any one can bring us to the brink of existential decision. Encounter with existence can come to individuals in many different ways. Even philosophy may serve as the occasion for such encounter, for some persons. So can the honest word of the poet, the irreparable loss of friendship or love, or the overflow of loving. But perhaps in our time, life in a dungeon, restrictions on freedom in Nazi-dominated France, or waiting to be incinerated in the ovens of Buchenwald have best served to awaken existing men to the realities of their existence. The average college boy, waiting to be called to give his life, if need be, for the causes of our day may also experience this *dénouement* of his being, whether he be American or Russian, African or Belgian.

But whatever the conditions under which we awaken from self-oblivion, senseless busyness, and triviality, though the awakening be painful, it is good. We can then at least distinguish between an individual existent pursuing tasks which relate, in turn, to deliberately chosen ends in a meaningful world upon which they depend for meaning, and an individual who must start from scratch because the existential posture which has overwhelmed him has put the task, the goal, the world, and his very being, into question. The gain is twofold: in perspective, and in the absolutely stripped character of the object which stands before vision, just as it is, whether it be existence or anything else. Under this posture we know that we *mean* something. We know, moreover, that our meaning has meaning of its own, which we cannot construct or merely project, but which we must discover, uncover, analyze, and describe. Under this posture we also know that our descriptions, analyses, and discoveries find their full meaning only in the light of what they can say about the existent being and his condition of being. (What otherwise could be the meaning and purpose of description, analysis, and discovery?) The purpose *for* which we even enact description, analysis, and discovery is here strictly scrutinized. They have to be accounted for in terms of what their enactor intends to say and do about himself and his condition of being. Describing, analyzing, and discovering are certainly purposive doings, yet they are done for a purpose which can be brought to light only as the purposer himself understands himself—what he is, and what he wants to be. The initiator of these projects finally gives meaning to their meaning. Men have always drawn accounts and descriptions of themselves and of their world, but not always have they included themselves in the accounts. The existentialist kind of account demands that the accounts, too, be accounted for, and that they be accounted for in terms of what they yield in the way of meaning to both the existing describer and analyzer and his world.

Let us now return to the position and existential posture of such a man as the butcher. Suppose we ask him the question, "What is art?" Let us suppose, further, that he is an aesthetically sensitive man, fully appreciative, even creatively capable of some one of the arts—say, poetry. We must also imagine, of course, that he is in full possession of the existential kind of reflection on art and on life generally to which his free posture in questioning now entitles him. We must suppose, for the sake of the illustration, that he has not gone so far as to have become an absolute and destructive nihilist who has altogether given up the quest for life's meaning. He has the intellectual capacity and sensitivities of a philosopher, a scientist, a religious man, and a poet, all put together, but we find him and address our question to him in the existential state in which he stands.

Admittedly, these suppositions are much too many for any single individual, but they illustrate fairly well the conditions under which the philosophical question about art or anything else has a reasonable chance for a direct and honest answer. A man like this is left with no external source of identity except what he himself represents, completely divested of all distracting ulterior motives and illusions. He now is in a position to make the search for life's meaning his real and serious business, taking precedence over any other. Any question that he may address to anything in his world, now, echoes a fundamental question about himself. The question itself, moreover, is for the sole purpose of achieving being and meaning as a being. He plays no mere role now; he has no audience to play up to, no reputation to defend, no ego.

How does art appear to the individual who has been shorn of all illusion? Why does this individual create or give his attention to art? How does he create or look at art? These are the questions to be asked here.

CHAPTER TWO

On the Object of Aesthetic Awareness

THE ART-OBJECT AS A FREE ESSENCE

We do not go to the concert in order to study the physics or the physiology of sound. Neither do we go to the museum in order to observe wood, canvas, pigments, or stone. We go to hear and to see what we call "works of art." As a matter of fact, we do not go to hear or to see anything in the same sense in which we go to see whether the lettuce has sprouted in our garden, or hear if the radio is on in the next room. Our general expectations, our orientations, are entirely different. We attend to a different sort of thing, and in fact "intend" a different kind of object, an object of our aesthetic awareness. Strictly speaking, the object we intend cannot even be said to exist: it both is and is not *there* coincidentally with the object of our ordinary perceiving awareness. *Hamlet* is not Laurence Olivier, and the *Mona Lisa* is not the thing subject to decay and change; yet it is Olivier's *Hamlet* that we see, and the *Mona Lisa* stands there before our very eyes.

The "time" and the "space" of the art-object are internal to it, cast once for all in an ideal form that the physical object of perception could never contain. Hamlet and all his utterances and actions remains in his own peculiar life-time and life-space, no matter how differently actors vary the presentation on the stage. The "time" of the symphony remains always the same, no matter how slow or how fast individual conductors may wish to render it.

A *lento* can be played faster without becoming an *allegro* and an *allegro* slower without becoming a *lento,* as long as the total *Gestalt* of the musical piece is respected (outside, or in violation of the *Gestalt,* the musical piece itself is no longer present). Michelangelo's *David* is eternally young. If the original of these art works were destroyed, any good reproduction would permit their re-enactment in our experience; their space-time-world was fixed once and for all by the will, the feeling, and the imagination of their creators.

The space and the time of an art-object are such as to remove this object from every condition and determination of historical reality, from what we call the real world. A vast and a small space in painting are quite the same for a miniature as for a large canvas; a small corner of a table, or a limitless desert scene can be effectively expressed in either. Though it may take an hour or more to present the play, the time of the dramatic action within the play runs its own independent course, and may even move backward as well as forward in time. The movement of a statue is unaffected by relocation of the statue; and a large or monumental horse may be only three inches high.

The sense in which the art-object is *in,* but not *of* historical reality makes of it a free object, unlike any other object that we can apprehend. It stands isolated, apart from the world of uncertain and precarious being. Utrillo's quiet Parisian scenes stand as if lifted above the tumult of the real world. So does Picasso's violent *Guernica.* In this respect, the object of aesthetic awareness appears to be extra- or super-phenomenal, having its being in a realm all its own, on its own conditions and terms. It stands peculiarly disengaged and freed from our practical and theoretical concerns. Mme. Bovary's conduct in Flaubert's novel is no one's business aside from the novel's own characters. No historical court could judge Hamlet to be, or not to be a murderer. Rubens' hefty nudes can offend the moral sensitivities only of the aesthetically obtuse. Only those whose eyes are closed to the aesthetic object can judge Di Chirico's ephemeral, dreamy horses solely for suitability to plowing, or declare Picasso's multi-nosed faces significantly in violation of the laws of biology. Only those who are victimized by logical compulsiveness judge Eliot's poem *The Waste Land* as nonsense.

The "is"s and the "is not"s, the "can"s and "cannot"s, the "do"s and the "don't"s, all are irrelevant to the art-object. We confront here a world where anything can be believed, said, and done, provided it is honestly felt and cast in presentative, child-like and uncalculating image. The world of the art-object is one in which no other rule holds than that of original, sincere realization, irrespective of purpose, of possible being as such. In this world, it is as pertinent to speak of Milton's "magnificent Satan" as of Della Robbia's "sweet bambinos"; of Lautrec's "fine prostitutes" as of Raphael's "beautiful madonnas," without getting involved with the way the world judges devils, bambinos, prostitutes or madonnas. The art-object represents a world whose being is prior to every form of judgment, and therefore immune to every judgment. Neither truth, nor goodness, nor any hypothetical imperatives measured by the practical and theoretical consciousness can touch it. This is a world in which the "good," the "true," and the "useful" are presented as pure possibilities, without intent to invalidate their opposites, which, too, may be so presented.[18] The art-object appears as a simple, direct presentation of possibility without practical or theoretical injunctions attached: it poses neither for what is, nor for what ought to be. It presents itself innocently and nakedly in the world of our existence without intent to embarrass or to build up our ordinary evaluations, though it can do this and more.

The peculiar composure and independence of the art-object come into clearer view when we see that it is in the order of a *presentation,* rather than a *re*-presentation. A representation, as the very word seems to say, presupposes another thing, somehow made to reappear under the guise of the art-object. A representation is unoriginal by definition. The essential characteristic of the art-object is precisely that it is an original—a *first* presentation of a possibility truly felt and imagined. It can remind us, really, only of itself,

---

[18] Although many philosophers have endeavored to establish the autonomy of art against moralistic, intellectualistic, and hedonistic interpretations, Benedetto Croce is no doubt responsible for the definitive modern work in this field. Croce's major works, which go under the title *Filosofia dello spirito,* have had one translation into English which, unfortunately, we hesitate to recommend to the student. Croce cannot be well translated literally, which is what usually is done. The student is, therefore, directed to the original Italian, *Estetica come scienza dell'espressione e linguistica generale* (Bari: Gius. Laterza e Figli, 1928). The student who does not read Italian will do well to read R. G. Collingwood, *The Principles of Art* (New York: Oxford University Press, 1958), which presents Croce's views much better than any translation of Croce does. For a general presentation of Croce's philosophy, see H. Wildon Carr, *The Philosophy of Benedetto Croce* (London: Macmillan & Co., 1927). See also Raffaello Piccoli, *Benedetto Croce: An Introduction to His Philosophy* (New York: Harcourt, Brace & World, 1922).

even if, in the process, we may remind ourselves of non-aesthetic things and events extraneous to it.

But though the art-object is, in the strict sense, not another object of the sort that go to make up the world, nor any copy or duplicate of such; though it stands neutral and apart from the spatio-temporal world, its mere presence, as we shall see in due course, can open our eyes to that real world as if we were seeing it for the first time. In this respect, its very firstness, innocence, ingenuousness, stands ever as a possibility for renewal or revision of our world and all its purposes. Like innocence itself, it can at times expose the banality or meaninglessness of some of our gravest projects, unmasking our most secret and guarded self-deceptions.

As pure presentation, the art-object remains unique, original, and unheard of. Perhaps it would be better to say that it is a *presence* rather than a presentation, since the latter word seems unavoidably to carry the sense that something is now being presented which had, or could have, some other kind of being in an unpresented state. The art presentation presents nothing that exists, has ever existed, or can exist. (How could Miró's *Little Fool in a Trance* exist?) If we said that it presents what it is possible to imagine, we would be all the more incorrect because so close, and yet so far, from the truth of the matter. The presentation is not a presentation *of* possibilities which might be said to subsist apart from the art-presence: the presence *is* the possibility itself—the whole of the being of it. Matisse's *Odalisque rouge* is all there is of the *Odalisque rouge*, the full fact of it. If this seems difficult to grasp, it is because more often than not we come to the art-object armed with abstract conceptual presuppositions regarding some realm of things that are imaginable and possible, and we read the aesthetic object as a presentation of one of these. In doing so, we surreptitiously slip the *conceptually possible* underneath or behind the art presence, pretending that it is now the appearance of one such kind. In this, we are incorrigible intellectual abstractionists, standing in the way of our own vision.

Only the unique, individual, and realized presence is aesthetically imaginable. Nothing that is *conceivable* is ever unique, individual, or realized as a presence like a work of art. If this were not so, we should be able to deduce the art object as we certainly can deduce the conceptually possible within any system of concepts. The idea or concept of a horse has nothing whatever in common with Di Chirico's horses. If they should relate in any way to the idea "horse," such idea would no longer be the object of a conceiving consciousness, but become entirely transmuted into image and feeling cast into aesthetic presence.

The art object is nothing but the present-felt-image, the realized possibility in all its uniqueness and individuality. Any actually imagined and felt presence of possible being is an art-object. Of the present possibility of being which the art-object constitutes, there can be none held in reserve, so to speak, and none can be unexpressed. It is this characteristic which led Benedetto Croce to say that people who believe they have poems or other art works "in their heads," but somehow just can't express them, are laboring under misapprehensions regarding both art and themselves. The art object cannot but be expressed—a presence, a monstrance—if it is to have any being at all.

But even as presence or monstrance, it shows up as a paradoxical being, for it is both something—a "what"—and nothing. The what of it is attested to by the fact that it is a presence; the nothingness, by the fact that it is not a presence of any thing. The unreality of the art-object is established on three counts: it is not a spatio-temporal object of our ordinary perceiving awareness; it is not any representation of such; and it is not something subsumed under any concept or system of concepts. It is easy and quite natural to say of a Di Chirico horse that it is something that doesn't exist, but quite a different matter to say what this means. How is it possible for the sheer presence of something that doesn't exist, and never can exist, to be something? To rest in the idea that it is a piece of imagination—a mere dream, a kind of hallucination—is to explain nothing. What is worse, such so-called explanations quickly and easily lend themselves to theoretical constructions which resolve the aesthetic phenomenon into psychologistic accounts at the service of practical or theoretical projects having little to do with the phenomenon itself.[19]

The paradox deepens when we consider that, although the aesthetic presence is not a presence of something other than itself, it cannot but be *for,* and present *to* a subject if it is to have any being at all. This observation indicates that the art-object can be objective precisely because its whole reference is to subjectivity. Its objectivity does not seem to rest on any necessary role it must play in the world of spatio-temporal things: the aesthetic object is not

[19] The Freudian approach to art is of this sort.

one included among the objects which constitute the world. Di Chirico's horses make no difference whatever to the physical universe. If a living man were not around to take notice of them, it would be as if they had never been—the world would not miss them. In this respect, the art-object is exactly like existing man himself: who, or what, would miss him or notice his absence if he had never been born? Like existence itself, the art-object is an appearance out of nowhere, a sudden invasion of the world. In contrast to the existing subject on whose very manner of being the art-object depends for its objectivity, however, it not only is a *what*—an essence—but an essence through-and-through. In this respect, it resembles less an existing man than it does a full-fledged object that needs neither time nor freedom to decide what meaning or essence it should have. The art-object is accomplished, all there, done. It is a thing freed of the necessity of having to live and to die.

As such, it makes its own demands, its own claims as a being, setting its own conditions for enactment at the very same time that it borrows its being and independence from the subject—that same subject whose own being is essence-less and in question. Thus the being of the art-object is, and must be, as precariously suspended on the abyss of being and nothingness as existing man himself is. The slightest turn in human interest and attention can reduce the *Mona Lisa* to a blur on a wall, Beethoven's *Ninth Symphony* to an irritating noise in the background of other, more urgent projects. The most aesthetically sensitive man is under no compulsion to lend beingness to the object whose very being as such depends on his tending to it. To put it another way, the object is grounded in a freedom for which it cannot but speak, even as it cannot but speak for itself as an independent phenomenon.[20]

For our present purposes, such observation can be taken to mean simply that the what or essence of the art-object is a *free* essence, founded on the free or spontaneous act of the subject-creator, born out of spontaneity itself. As an essence, it is no part of any system of essences, either of the "real" world, or of any conceptually deduced world. It stands as witness to the presence of spontaneous and free being in the midst of a world which resists and limits it. The radical freedom upon which it rests and to which it refers is such that this object itself does not depend for its being on any system

[20] See Chapter Two.

of cohering objects of its own kind. Leonardo's *Last Supper* did
not necessarily have to be just because the *Mona Lisa* had come
into being. Each work of art is unique, unpredictable, unrelated to
any other. Often the works of a single artist display as much difference from one to another as those of different artists working in
different epochs. (Compare Picasso's classical with his cubistic
periods.) All truly significant unifying characteristics speak, not so
much for similarities among the objects themselves, as for the endeavor at self-unity of their subject-creators. We give recognition
to this fact in the very way we speak of the period to which this or
that work of a certain artist belongs—the so-called blue, and pink
periods of Picasso, for instance. Any important discussion of such
periods cannot be based solely on external observations and gen-
eralizations of certain features of the art-object; it must relate to
the creator's own struggle to "find himself," as it is said, with all
that this involves. In this deeper sense, similarities in the art
presence often bridge one epoch with another without regard to
chronological sequence or the individuality of the artist. For instance, much that Rouault has done bears greater affinity, in a way,
to medieval than to contemporary aesthetic sensitivity. The Super-
man that Nietzsche so passionately sang about bears a greater resemblance to the man of Aristotle than to that of either Heidegger
or Sartre.[21] It is the existential effort of the existent to make for
himself a meaning out of nothing that accounts for the likenesses
among his own works, and for the likeness that his work may bear
to the works of other existents, no matter when or where they
lived.

The world of art-objects is a world of independent essences, related only to and by the subjectivity which calls them into being,
and which sustains them in being. As a free essence, the art-object
always presents a possible-self-in-a-possible-world, publicly put forth
on its own account as a possibility of being.[22] (It must be remembered that only linguistic necessity makes us say that "it presents"
such possibility; the reader must keep in mind that the aesthetic
presence *is* the possibility, just as it stands.) Metaphysical speculations attest to the rational and conceptual capacity of the existent
to set up rational possible being. But such being, as Kierkegaard
clearly saw, must always remain unpresent—and, in this sense, un-

[21] Walter Kaufmann, *Existentialism from Shakespeare to Sartre* (New York:
Doubleday & Co., 1960), pp. 1-24.
[22] See Chapter Two.

realized—possibility.[23] In the art-object, the envisioned possibility is so fully realized that it is made as present as existence itself. We can consider Aquinas' intellectual view of man and his world as a conceptual possibility of being—surely then, Dante's aesthetic realization of it in the *Divine Comedy* is the thing that permits us to live it and to live in it with feeling and imagination, in a way that no purely conceptual construction could ever do. It is not true that the *Divine Comedy* makes no claims for the truth-value of the vision which it represents, a contrast with St. Thomas' claims for his propositions. The *Divine Comedy*'s truth needs no other inward confirmation than that which it generates by its very presence as feeling and imagination. This is a *truthfulness* grasped—stopped in its tracks, as it were—cast in an eternal immediacy which admits of no doubts or invidious comparisons. Of course, such truth settles none of our practical and theoretical problems and uncertainties but what we must note is that what it settles aesthetically, it *really* settles once and for all. No aesthetically sensitive man would think of bringing the astronomy or the psychology of the *Divine Comedy* up to date. For the *Divine Comedy,* Ptolemaic astronomy and medieval psychology are absolutely true. The Archbishop Ruggiero forever must gnaw at the skull of Count Ugolino, and Paolo compulsively be driven by passion and unappeasable hunger after Francesca. The truth of the *Divine Comedy* is self-enclosed, settled in a clear and fully discovered way of feeling and imagining which makes the possibility into a presence. Doubts do not disturb it.

LOGICAL, REAL, AND AESTHETIC ORDERS

Necessitated by nothing except subjective spontaneity itself, the art-object nonetheless carries the most rigorous necessity within its own internal constitution. We must establish this peculiar kind of internal necessity by way of contrast with other forms of necessitation, from which it is excluded. The sense in which it is free cannot otherwise be established. Let us contrast it with logical and real orders.

As any student of logic knows, the necessity and unity which obtains in any logical system of concepts is such that one thing is

[23] Robert Bretall, ed., *A Kierkegaard Anthology* (Princeton: Princeton University Press, 1947), p. 134.

contained in, derived from, and consequent to another. The whole as well as the parts of such systems live an abstract, unpresent life, nowhere making a unique individual and actual showing. The essential nature of the system is to be, not monstrance, but demonstration. If presentational immediacy of any kind can be associated with it, it must be either in the primitive elements on which its whole internal order rests (elements often called "self-evident") or on the aesthetic feeling of the system as a whole; but both of these fall outside the system itself. Even if they lend the system all the necessitation it possesses, they are not necessitated *by* the system, being an aesthetic rather than an intellectual or conceptual matter. The system's necessitating or cohering power operates unseen, from behind the world of thoughts which it binds together. The unifying element remains anonymous, never revealing anything of the existent who initiates it as a project. The project of the rational system, as a matter of fact, becomes initiated on condition that its ties with the existent be severed. More than this, in making its claims, the system must of necessity pose as subject-less—it must be a proclamation of an impersonal "Reason." It speaks, not for the being who sets it up, but only for the project which this being initiates by setting up the system. Hence it can never contain the free agent who makes it or finds need to make it.

In contrast, the order or necessitation which can be observed in the art-object seems to be instituted, not for the purpose of setting up some kind of truth or achieving a practical end, but simply *to tell the truth* about how the existent feels and imagines existence itself, apart from any and all projects initiated to carry out a life. In other words, the life-project that the art-object exhibits has nothing to do with supporting any of the projects by which the existent intends to further his causes. He acts independently of both theoretical and practical commitment, attending simply and directly to the spontaneity or freedom that he embodies. Because of this radical disengagement, spontaneity is exhibited in the art-object as *indifferently* purposing any or all values—including the value we call truth—freely, as a possibility, independent of anything that theory or practice demand in their own right. The art-object thus stands as a symbol of the self-deliverance of the existent. To put it another way, it stands as his endeavor to carry on these same projects, not unself-consciously, but in the very presence of his own self-transcending freedom—a being forever ahead of himself, always more than he is, and never what he ought or must be. The art-object stands as a symbol of the existent's own need and yearning for being, and not for carrying on a life. Therefore, it presents pure possibilities of being fashioned in, for, by, and of spontaneity itself.

For this reason, the kind of necessary order or necessitation inherent in the art-object is not one of sequential and implicative being, but one in which the relation of *compresence* is realized. This is a relation in which everything is both necessitated and unnecessitated, depending on how one chooses to look at it. The art-object offers neither truth, goodness, nor profit, as these values are measured in the world—it offers only a clear vision of the joy, the despair, the mystery, and the possibility of meaning or of meaninglessness of our existence. It also shows that whatever existence must be, or whatever its true and final meaning, it can at least be tasted now, intimately owned, lived through, even if just as a possibility of being, joyous, tragic, or comical. Under the state in which existence can be said to be naked, divested of all pretensions at its origins, it would be a fulfillment to learn by some immediate disclosure that it was at least tragic or even something just comical or meaningless altogether. The art-object presents these possibilities, though it does not propose them as real or necessary. It confirms nothing, except, perhaps, that being must be lived as we live our very own present existences before it can have any sense or meaning *for us.*

The relation of compresence as among the parts and the whole of the art-object is in no way similar to the relation which obtains between the whole and the parts of any conceptual or logical system. The parts (if parts they can be called) do not follow one another sequentially in the whole, but constitute microcosms of the presence of the whole whose presence, in turn, can be accounted for only as the parts themselves are, remaining present in and with it. The necessity of the art-object, internally considered, derives from the inter-presence of the parts in the whole. Neither the parts nor the whole make any appearance whatever independently of one another. They come into their presences together, and together also with the existent who is witness to their being. They confirm their separate and related beings in the presence and realization of one another, even as the existent for whom they have their being confirms them as possible being in the light of his own being which is present in itself in a way that no conceptual system could ever be. The art-object is present as a whole to the existent in a way that rational and real objects never are. The objects of the rational and deductive consciousness take their leave, one after the other, as they pay tribute to an unseen necessity which draws them one out of the other in order to reach a whole which never can have actual, unique and individual presence. Those of the aesthetic presentation require one another's presence in the whole as prerequisites to a sense of presence, and to give presence to the whole. In its aesthetic meaning, a single form in, say, a Cézanne still-life is derived neither from the whole nor from the forms in the whole, but constitutes, and is in turn constituted by, the whole and every other part which shows up as present or actual in itself. The art object is thus a mirror of its creator, who is or seeks to be, not many, but a single being, and wholly present.

The reader may, perhaps, better concretize for himself this relationship of compresence in the aesthetic object, if, with some actual art-object before him, he imagines himself pulling out some line, shape, or form from the whole, watching to see what would happen to both the part and the remaining whole. He would find in both a character entirely different from that which they possessed before their separation—the experiment would work as well with any form of art besides a painting.

So much for the contrast between conceptual and aesthetic orders. A glance at the contrast between real and aesthetic orders reveals other radical differences. In the world, things stand adjacent to, but in exclusion of one another, and their temporal endurance is by substitution. Every object excludes every other object; every entity persists by a kind of prolonged dying. The only necessity in this realm seems to be one of separateness, of passing into other things or out of being altogether. Everything remains outside of everything else, but, paradoxically, everything also passes into other things, or into nothing. The world of spatio-temporal things displays a ubiquitous individuality or uniqueness of sorts, but this is an individuality either entirely devoid of inwardness or "inside," or else concealing it as something epiphenomenal, insubstantial, fatuous, unreal. In this order, nothing ever achieves full self-presence, nothing escapes the annihilation of time. The only permanence is in a sepulchral, ever-fading memory of "having been." In contrast to this order of isolation and death, the order of the art-object is one in which everything is preserved in its being, everything achieves actual presence together with everything else, and everything relates and refers to an existent. Everything in the art-object stands fully realized, unchanging, and in full view. Nothing is inessential, everything is required. A single line, a dab of color, a sound—all are constitutive and uneliminable from the whole. Their relationship to other lines, colors, or sounds as well as to the whole is never one of mere adjacency, correlation, or probability.

The unity and internal necessity of the art-object clearly has no parallel in the world of things or of thoughts. We can say of this unity that it is unity *par excellence*—*necessitation without necessity*. And no wonder. It is exclusively the spontaneity of the subject that binds it in the free essence which it is. To understand this kind of unity and necessitation we have to turn our attention to the existent himself, for the unity consists basically of an indissoluble union of feeling and image with the sense of self-identity. There seems to be no other way of accounting for the compresence of parts and whole in the art object. The unique feeling which binds and holds everything compresent is cast once and for all in an immutable image in such a way that the feeling becomes the image, the image the feeling, of him who feels and imagines. But for all this, the feeling does not lose its character as feeling, nor the image its character as image. Each takes on the character of the other while retaining its own. In this peculiar interpenetration, feeling achieves actual self-presence or expression for the subject, and image achieves inward subjective content. In this way, the object can be the *utterance*—the *spoken word* of the subject—and the subject can come into possession of his own utterance, disclosing himself to himself as a spontaneity. The unity of an aesthetic object, in other words, represents the unification of the subject himself, insofar as he achieves self-liberation and self-consciousness of being as he honestly confesses and names his own feelings to himself. This constitutes at once a free positing and affirmation of the spontaneity that the subject himself is, and a projecting self-transcendence into pure possibility of self and world combined.

SUBJECTIVITY AND THE ART-OBJECT

Considered as felt-image or imaged-feeling, the free essence of the art-object begins to display more clearly its own unique structure, both as a subjective and an objective thing. As a subjective or spontaneous thing, it appears to be spontaneity's self-expression, pure and simple. As an objective thing, it seems to be the self-expression or exhibit-to-itself of the same spontaneity. ("Expressed" here has the sense of "pressed out" or "thrown out into the open," and "imaged" or "imagined" has the sense of "made into an articulate, independent presentation.") The art-object thus stands before us as both fact and spontaneous act in one. Both self and world thus are emancipated and returned to the spontaneous ground which is the source of their experiential concreteness for the existent.

Not all feeling becomes expressed in aesthetic image, and not all imagining is purposed to make feeling into a presence. Most feeling, in fact, translates itself directly into action, and most imagining is for inventive anticipatory action, or else for vicarious living. In such cases, feeling and imagination are, in one form or another, simply adjuncts to action, spontaneity and effort being spent to purchase gains or ends which are non-aesthetic in nature.[24]

Feeling and imagination are joined in such a way that the image is felt and the feeling is imagined, and our encounters with art-objects are more like encounters with people than with things. A dialogue of a sort, a certain mutuality of self-disclosure is made possible. We betray recognition of this when we speak of "going to see a Matisse," or "going to hear Beethoven." The work of art is always somebody's, something tied inseparably to personality, even if its creator remains unknown to us.[25] Somehow, it always announces personal spontaneous existence—even if it be only a specially selected but unmodified piece of driftwood, the fact that it has been chosen by some sensitive, feeling, and imaginative person, gives it the stamp of personality, thus transforming it into felt-image. Discriminating selection marks it as a product of spontaneity, lifting it out of the realm of mere things and giving it the afflatus of personality and universality. Driftwood offers an illustration telling us something fundamental about the relation between the artist's materials and the aesthetic object he impresses on them. It tells us much more, in fact; it suggests a whole new way of looking at the relation between art and what we call "nature." For, in the artist's

[24] The distinction derives from the position taken throughout this study that the essential character of purposing activity cannot be determined by appearance alone; thus, image-making is involved in vicarious and inventive imagination as well as in the aesthetic.

[25] Sartre, L'Être et le néant (Paris: Bibliothèque des idées), pp. 115-150.

work we have a prototype of what might be called the *humanization of nature* or of the thing, a phenomenon pervasive in human experience. Reaching from its own depths, spontaneous personality puts its imprint on natural things resolving them into its own unsubstantial kind of being, and entirely appropriating them as carrier and record of its visions of the possible.[26] In this way, the ideal and the possible are not merely attached to the real and the actual, but are themselves brought to reality and actuality by an act of transmutation in which natural things are annulled as such and made to speak anew, affirmed anew in their being. The voice and the being, however, are now those of the existent. To see the art-object, one must be able to *not see* the world. To see the *Mona Lisa,* one must be able to *not see* the wood, the paint, and the canvas as such; to hear the music, one must be able to *not hear* the sounds as sounds; to see *Hamlet,* one must be able to *not see* the stage as stage, *not see* Laurence Olivier as Laurence Olivier. The urgency of this creative nihilation and novel imprinting of nature obtains whether we be the artist making the art-object, or appreciators re-enacting it for ourselves. It is not sufficient to say that we merely forget, or put aside all attention to the wood, the paint, the sound, the real Laurence Olivier. The phenomenon of the enactment of the art-object involves something more dynamic which enters directly into its constitution. The artist wrestles with his materials, struggles to make them disappear as such, so that they can speak his word—*only his word.* The materials are put to the service of the artist's aesthetic vision only as they can be resolved into his own spontaneity.

Feeling and image are so perfectly and completely resolved into one another in the art-object that absolute lucidity of meaning results. The object's being and its reason for being are there with the presence in full view, concealing nothing. Everything that the object is stands openly before us in a here-and-now which, unlike the moment of time and the places of our existence, is not burdened by pasts to overcome and futures to gain. Both time and space are converted into fluid possibility, at the complete disposal of the spontaneous subject. Immanuel Kant said of the art-object that it represented the work of a "purposiveness without purpose." [27] It instigates nothing, replaces nothing, proves nothing, pretends noth-

---

[26] See Chapter Four.

[27] Kant, *Critique of Aesthetic Judgement* (London: Oxford University Press, 1911), p. 43.

ing. The art-object is artless as only authentic innocence and in-genuousness can be.

But child-like candor must not be confused with superficiality or the trivial. The art-object has the ingenuousness of a first vision of things, but of necessity carries also the demonic, deep soundings of groundless spontaneity itself, out of which it is born and by which it is sustained in being.[28] Its very unpremeditatedness and complete openness of being give it a peculiar inexhaustibility of meaning, and make it at times something not altogether safe to have around. Both of these characteristics, which seem to conflict with its openness and purposelessness, derive from the fact that this object is a free essence, grounded only in groundless freedom itself. With that freedom, it shares a dangerous, a precarious position on the brink of nothingness—that Nothingness of which Paul Claudel asks, "Is it nothing, that Nothingness which delivers us from everything?" The fact alone that the art-object presents free possibilities of being, of both self and world, *indifferently,* establishes the exact sense of its depth and demonic character.[29]

Though unique, unrepeatable, alone of its kind, the art presence remains a source of novel being which fixes an infinity of things and states under its own distinctive single mode of feeling and imaging. Hence it is always infinitely more of itself, of its own kind of being, than can be explored and charted on any single encounter. It stands as a prototype of a possibility of being. Its limits are none other than the limits of spontaneous feeling and imagination itself.

This explains how it is possible for us to "enter" into the "world" of Piero della Francesca, Van Gogh, César Franck, through the portals of their particular works. Once in these worlds, we find ourselves, in terms of spontaneous feeling and of imagining, able to see a universe; the possibilities inherent within the single possibility unfold effortlessly, invitingly, even irresistibly. They can even overflow, spill over the bounds of the art-object as such and into the world of our existence (they are, in fact, always ready to do this). It is then that the nondescript landscape we daily look upon through the livingroom window suddenly takes on the distinct quality and characteristics of a Cézanne painting, becoming "visible" to us for the first time. It is then, too, that the vicissitudes of our puny, inconsequential existence may take on either the majesty of Homeric epic or Shakespearean tragedy, or at the very least presenta-

[28] Nietzsche, *The Birth of Tragedy* (New York: Doubleday & Co., 1956), p. 29.
[29] See pp. 52-56.

tion of the Absurd like that of Kafka or Camus. Even the meaning that is called "meaninglessness," when afforded to our existence by such overflowings, can open our eyes to authenticity and unauthenticity of living, which is a kind of meaning all its own.

It is precisely because of these possibilities that, although in itself innocuous, unpremeditated, removed from the world, the art-object nonetheless stands ever as a threat to any and all espoused causes, to all purpose doggedly engaged where the existent and his groundless freedom are forgotten or fall out of concern. Plato understood well that the aesthetic element is not irrelevant to its potentially revolutionary import, that art can put the value of truth and of being itself into question. For art is the ontologically free venture of the existent, ever attesting to the fact that no philosophy and no program of action can contain a man unless he first makes himself into a thing that can be so contained. The existent can contain these things but cannot be contained by them in turn, for he is always in excess of them—he is nothing; and as nothing, not to be contained in anything.

ART, DREAM, AND SPONTANEITY

If we seek for an object which resembles the art-object, we will find none better than the dream. Not only does the dream-construct resemble the art-construct, but the dreaming consciousness itself exhibits unmistakable similarities to the aesthetic consciousness. The similarities, in fact, are so striking that a phenomenology of the dream seems to tie in with a phenomenology of art. We cannot here, of course, venture into this nearly virgin territory except briefly, and only then to suggest some of the more obvious comparisons.[30]

In both the art and the dream phenomena there is clearly exhibited a consciousness which works freely or spontaneously to

[30] Despite the enormous literature on dreams, little or nothing has so far been done by way of phenomenological research in this field. See Jean Hering, "Quelques thèmes d'une phénoménologie de rêve," in *Nine Essays in Phenomenology*, p. 75; also by the same author, "Concerning Image, Idea, and Dream" in *Philosophy and Phenomenological Research* (December 1947), pp. 188-205. The most important studies of the dream and art images remain those in Jean-Paul Sartre, *The Psychology of Imagination* (New York: The Citadel Press, 1961), pp. 231, 273.

produce or enact self-contained presentations. In both, a productive consciousness is free and disengaged from practical and theoretical purposings, while the constructs are internally necessitated in their own peculiar way. In this respect, both differ in the same way from wakeful activity or real life, which exhibits a structure that is the exact reverse of this. In the waking state, activity-as-a-whole is unfree—bound to tasks, pervasively care-full, as Heidegger has said. But its particular projects everywhere rest on choice and decision, which entail (under conditions of authentic existence at least) dreadful responsibility as well as uncertainty. We choose neither our existence nor the world, even though we remain free to commit suicide, or change our surroundings in limited ways, at any moment. In the dream as in art, life and the world are projects founded on a spontaneity which sustains them in being. Things do not have to appear or to happen as the theoretical and practical consciousness requires. Time can move backward, forward, or not at all; spatial orderings are determined by spontaneous feeling and imagination alone. In art as in dreaming we can "die" and "live again" many times over, even within a single dream or single play, as the case may be. However internally necessitated, the individual project itself has here no other necessitation than spontaneity itself.

Both the aesthetic and the dreaming consciousness thus speak for a spontaneity of being which comes into possession of itself, and is capable of throwing itself or casting itself into possible-existence-in-the-world, whereas the consciousness-as-a-whole of wakeful existence speaks for a spontaneity which is thrown or cast into the world by no determination of its own. Hence, in the aesthetic and dreaming consciousness, the individual projects are complete and accomplished possibilities wherein the spontaneity which engenders them can live as a whole. In the waking consciousness, the spontaneity remains homeless and unaccomplished in every one of its projects, which perforce must remain uncompleted.

The contrast of these structures suggests, in the comparison, a relation of complementarity between dream and art, on the one hand, and existence-in-the-world on the other. It suggests that existence-in-the-world may hold in its depths a nostalgic yearning to be like the dream, or like art, insofar as its root-spontaneity could become via these creations self-possessed and reality-making on its own as a being. It suggests further that the dreaming and aesthetic consciousnesses can express, in turn, a yearning to establish and fulfill that spontaneity in actuality freed from all limits, including the limit of death itself. Of course, we can no more live life by dreaming it, or by aesthetically feeling and imagining it, than we can transmute it at will into the free essence of the art-object or the dream. Only in those rare moments of absolute spontaneity, in which every last trace of conflict and obstruction to purposing seem to have left us, do we momentarily experience some sense of this incredible possibility.[31]

The phenomena of the constructs or objects wrought by the dreaming as by the aesthetic consciousness, are remarkably similar. Like the art-object, the dream exhibits the characteristics of a pure presentation, a free essence, a felt image or imaged-feeling. It stands, Janus-faced, referring to a subjectivity whose spontaneous depths it discloses in child-like candor, and yet to an observable world of images, which stand objectively before the intentional consciousness of the dreamer. Like the art-object, the dream-object is not something that can be deduced or inferred either from conceptual schemes or from the system of the waking-state world. It has the same kind of uniqueness and individuality as the work of art. Like the work of art, the dream stands related to the subject-dreamer alone, necessitated only by the unnecessitated spontaneity who is the dreamer himself. No particular dream is implicit in, or derivable from any other dream in any necessary way.

The very mode of being of the dream-object is, like the art-object, to be nothing—*no thing*. Although it might appear that the dream-object, in contrast to the art-object, lacks embodiment in the substance of the waking-state world, this is not really the case. The embodiment, the vehicle, the mnemonic carrier of the dream, is drawn from waking-state experience held in whatever memory of wakeful life is operative in the dreaming state. Moreover, the relationship between such "materials" and the constructive dreaming consciousness appears to be quite the same as that between the perceptual materials of ordinary consciousness and the productive aesthetic activity upon which it works. Remembered perceptual experience becomes annulled as such, while it is being transformed into the substance of the felt image of the dream.

The same interpenetration of feeling and image obtains in the dream as in the art-object. The unity of the dream is a unity of compresent parts, each feeding meaning to all other parts and to the whole, which in turn feeds meaning to all the parts. This is a characteristic well known to the psychiatrist. But even beyond this

[31] The yearned-after experience of the mystics may be of this sort.

self-presence, wherein the dream speaks as a whole at the same time that it speaks in its parts, the characteristic of inexhaustibility we noted to be present in the art-object is present here, also. Though the dream is all present, in full view and put forth with absolute candor, every word spoken in it, every event, every object means more than is shown. The dream presents a prototype of possible-self-and-its-world, open for exploration in depth, with reference both to the subject's own condition of being, and to the possible kind of world it presents. Some dreams are like paintings or tableaux; others, more like plays. Others are much like musical compositions in that the course and development of a certain mood or feeling seems mostly to be what constitutes them.

The dream shares with the work of art also a latent power to transform or change existence at its roots—it carries revolutionary import. But of this, history and contemporary psychiatry tell the story much better than we could ever do here.[32]

There remains one last phenomenological consideration to make. The dream is something one remembers, and remembers, moreover, as his own dream. In this respect, the dream is first known in our waking experience as everything else that is and must be remembered, whether dream or not. I remember my dream of having met a friend in no way differently than I remember having really met my friend yesterday. My existence in time is so constituted that absolutely nothing that happens, outside of the instant when it is actually happening, can be present and recognized as happening, and as happening to me, except in a present memory. From this standpoint, both wakeful experience and dream-experience stand on exactly the same footing: I encounter them in a present memory. However, when I remember having met with my friend yesterday in what we call "real life," I also seem to "remember," together with what happened, the state itself of being wakeful and attending to the real business of living. The fact that it happened while I was awake and engaged in actual living I do not have to infer from a comparison with dream occurrences (there is nothing else I could compare it with). Together with the memory of the real event, I seem to recover also the sense of what it is like for me to be in the state of wakeful living. The point is that the memory of any real happening entails the recovery also of a memory in which the continuity of wakeful living is sustained in a present *now* of wakeful

---

[32] The role of dream-interpretation in psychiatry is well known; also, note dreams like those of Constantine which influenced the course of human history.

existence. How must a being be constituted so that the present memory of any real and actual event can be possible? The answer surely must include recognition of some kind of memory of the state in which the remembered event took place. More than this, such memory would have to be the memory of *what it is like* to enact such a state. From this perspective, except for the present moment of actual enactment or active involvement, existence in the world is, in the particulars and as a whole, a memory of having been joined to an active memory of what it is like to be under a certain mode or state of being.

But when I remember my dream, do I also remember the mode or state of my being under which I enacted the dream? If I do, how is this possible? Forgetting for the moment those rare cases when I am somehow awake and dreaming at the same time, it appears that when I am dreaming I am dead to the waking state; awake, I am dead to the dreaming state. No memory of my self and my world appears to be operative in any sense of "memory" that I can recognize in my waking state: the memory of memory seems to be gone. How do I know that what I remember happened only in a dream, and not really? If we say that I know this by some quick comparison of the dream events with the waking-state events as I awake, I still cannot explain how it is that many dreams which I remember long after awakening often present no particular or startling contrast with my waking-state surroundings and its actual doings. I do not, in such cases, *deduce* that the dream was a dream. I seem to *know* it, directly, as if I had some way of visiting while awake the actual state in which dreams are created. A certain memory of what it is like to dream comes with the memory of the dream itself. I am as certain that what I remember happening in the dream happened while I was dreaming as I am that what I remember as really happening really happened while I was going about the business of wakeful living. My essential capacity to recognize and to immediately discriminate each state for what it is does not always seem to depend on any comparisons that I make between them. Phenomenologically considered, both states and their respective appearances are like familiar places which I visit, while yet remaining in some profound aspect of my own being free and independent of both, and capable, moreover, of remembering myself as a spontaneity that can move in and out of both projects.

It appears, however, that I can no more enter into or enact the state of dreaming at will than I can while dreaming hold on to my awareness and memory of the way of remembering required to carry on wakeful projects. If a memory of self as enactor of both states be possible, neither state would seem to contain this remembered self in such a way that I can clearly own it in either state considered in itself. Such a self, as spontaneity capable of either enactments, seems like a vagrant being who enacts, but also escapes, all of its states and projects while living in and through them all. Neither dream nor actual existence seem to contain it within their own proper domain. In neither does there seem to be full self-recognition and self-possession of the spontaneity which underlies them both. We enter and depart from both wakeful living and dreaming as from two separate worlds to which we are strangers in our very depths.

Something in me dreams and permits me to speak to my self in dreams, and the same thing lives and permits me to speak to and about my self in the way of wakeful presentations. Both worlds present themselves as incarnate symbolizations of what we are, what we need, what we pretend to be in order to be. Both dreaming and living exhibit the character of a pathetic effort to speak the first word about, or to give name to the being that we are in our existential depths.[33]

The art-object is like the dream-object; the state of consciousness which stands behind it is like the dreaming consciousness, but with a telling, all-important difference. In art, it is as if the spontaneity which stands behind or underneath both living and dreaming were capable of living and enacting itself in both simultaneously, achieving a degree of self-possession and self-conscious enactment in a *now* that transcends the actuality and the *now* of both. The phenomenon of remembering a dream and what it is like to dream bears startling similarity to the way we are able to enact the aesthetic presence and to move in and out of its "world." But in art, the memory of the spontaneity that we are *almost* bridges the gap between dreaming life and living it. The sense in which art is like a dream which must be enacted in the living world in order that the actor's self may be enacted in it is readily illustrated: we need only remember those occasions when we have stood beside someone looking at a work of art, giving every evidence of "seeing" or experiencing something, while we have stood by wondering what on earth that person was seeing and experiencing that so eluded us. Granting that the other person was not faking, our

[33] See Chapter Four.

difficulty was an inability to "dream" while awake. The aesthetic consciousness is enacted in interpenetrating waking-dreaming states, accelerated to the point of instantaneous activity in which we dream while awake. Hence, we are neither exclusively dreaming nor exclusively awake, but rather are joined to that root spontaneity of our existential being which lives in both states, and which transcends both.

In certain respects, dreaming and its constructs are more like life than art; in certain respects the aesthetic consciousness and its objects are more like dreaming and the dream than like life. In other respects, dreaming and the dream more nearly resemble art than life; aesthetic consciousness and its products resembles life more than dreaming and the dream. In the art-object, the spontaneity of our existence seems to be in command of both dreaming and living, establishing itself paramount to both in what Benedetto Croce has called "the dream of the life of cognition," a position in being from which we "stand as if in the very presence of the creation of the world." But perhaps, rather than speak of a surpassing of life and of dreaming, we ought to speak of a return, a *ricorso*, as Giambattista Vico suggests, to our very origins, to our own spontaneous depths, where resides the source of our sense of every mode of being, and where spontaneity itself is replenished. The aesthetic consciousness and its object would thus be the renewers and restorers of our strength and courage to be, and to create values.[34]

[34] See pp. 109-120.

CHAPTER THREE

Common Elements & Structures

in Art & Life

ON THE CONCRETE ELEMENTS

We have now to examine the art-object as a work of execution, how it is put together, and what the elements or parts are which are put together in the indissoluble unity so peculiar to art. We begin by noting that just as it is not the art-object which a mover engaged to transport paintings or sculpture from one place to another carries out to his truck, neither are the constituent elements and their unity in the art-object objects of ordinary perceptive awareness.

In a drawing, lines are not merely the shortest distances between points; in a sculpture, mass and volume are not the same mass and volume with which physics is concerned. In the drama, action is not the same as the behavior that the psychologist studies. Such elements of the art-object are, like the object itself, things felt and imagined —felt because cast in image, and images because felt as such. Lines in a painting are "calmly flowing," "violent," "strong," and "gentle"; masses in a piece of sculpture are "heavy" or "light"; and so on. The colors in a painting are not the same thing as the stuff packed in tubes. Let us explain this statement as representative example for any and all art elements, *mutatis mutandi*.

In the sense in which it is aesthetically significant, a dab of the material from a tube becomes color only when it is placed on the canvas. Only then does it emerge as a color uniquely felt in relation to other colors and to the color of the canvas itself. Until then, it is indeterminate, artistically speaking. Two dabs of different stuffs juxtaposed but not blended change one another qualitatively so that different values, intensities, and even different hues (color qualities) result. The same occurs when they are blended. There is no color, in the aesthetic sense, except as color arises in the *Gestalt*, or, more precisely, except as the *Gestalt* or whole aesthetic presence itself is in process of arising. What is in the tube can be almost anything, and there is no way of determining in any concrete way what color it is prior to its emergence or felt-imaged presence in the work of art. In a sense, for all aesthetic purposes, the stuff in the tube must be made to "disappear" as such before any aesthetically significant color can appear. This is why an artist paints, not from the tubes, but from a palette. The artist's palette is no merely physical and impersonal thing: it is a sort of magical laboratory, where the aesthetically neutral or indeterminate stuff from the tubes is transmuted into color in the aesthetic sense. The palette is thus a field of operation in which is included the canvas and everything else entering into the process of expression. Even when an artist seems not to go through the overt performance of setting up a palette in the sense of mixing pigments on a separate surface, his true palette remains the art construct itself in process of taking form. If he applies pigment directly from tube onto canvas, the artist remains in the presence of the total effect that is emerging within him as well as before him. The very movements of his body, as these are internally and kinaesthetically present to him, enter constitutively into this concrete, total, and organic act of stamping a name on his own feelings. The total process is no mechanical activity wherein he arranges, orders, or combines things already given. The presence of the elements or parts of the work of art must be made to emerge as the presence as a whole emerges.[35]

It is appropriate at this point to take note of a common misconception with regard to both the execution and the analysis of the work of art in relation to its elements or component parts. Just as we mistakenly think of the painter as putting together or organizing certain given or pre-existing materials in constructing his work, so also do we think of the poet as first gathering certain dictionary-words and "ideas" which he afterwards "puts together" in order to produce a poem. We conceive of the execution of a work of art much as we conceive of the mechanic at his work, or the carpenter

[35] Croce, *Estetica*, pp. 5-6.

at his. The artist, we believe, starts with an "idea," a plan, an end to be realized, and then proceeds to gather and manipulate materials, whatever they may be, to manufacture a planned product. We carry this same prejudice into our intentional posture when we confront the work of art in order to critically analyze it, or simply to appreciate it (re-create it in our own way). We seek to discover or to re-enact some adequateness of means to an end, which we suppose is what the artist attempted to do.[36]

The misconception is radical. It prevents us from seeing the work of art as well as its elements. As was pointed out earlier, art is a purposiveness without purpose, a purposing freed from all projects which must be such that the end to be achieved antecedes, or can be distinguished in thought from the means and process of achieving it. The painting, the poem, the musical composition, together with their elements, do not exist before they appear: the creator of these things cannot pre-view them, or plan them in advance. They arise in the act of their execution, and their creator meets with them as they emerge in the process in which they are wrought. Picasso cannot predict what work he will produce next—the work of art which he will next produce will, when he has given birth to it, be as much of a revelation, a surprise, an absolutely novel disclosure to him as to anybody else. If this were not the case, great art could be produced at will. We could then gather sure figures on how many works of art would be produced within the coming year, saying even what they would be like, by simply asking our artists how many works they intended to produce for the year, and what "ideas" they were thinking of expressing. As a matter of fact, the elements of art and the rules for arranging them could be reduced to a formula, available to anybody who had an "idea" he wanted to express. We could manufacture art on the assembly line.

Just as the whole of the aesthetic presence is a free essence, sustained in being by the spontaneity of the existent, so also its elements and constituent parts have no being outside of the act which lends them felt-imaged—objectivity. Everything that has so far been observed with respect to the object of aesthetic awareness applies equally to the elements of the object. Lines, spaces, shapes, textures, and colors in all their dimensions in painting; mass, volume, movements, shapes and textures in sculpture; patterns of movement in the dance; and so on for every form of aesthetic expression have to do with constituents which cannot be found out-

[36] Collingwood, *The Principles of Art,* pp. 20-41.

side of the work of art considered as an ideal object. The elements of the art-object, too, speak for the spontaneous ground of existence —for the existent, in the spontaneity of his essential being. They stand to the free utterance of art-objects as component words stand to a complete sentence in ordinary discourse. They constitute a vocabulary, so to speak, of elemental felt-images, whose realized presences enter constitutively into the realized presence which is the art-object as a whole. The relationship that they bear to the brute sense-materials (pigments, soundwaves, words, the theories of the theoretical consciousness, historical actions, and so on) is one in which feeling and image pass from an obscure unself-possessed, existentially dumb and un-named state to one in which the existent can speak and disclose his feelings to himself. The relation is one of conquest, of resolution of the inert and voiceless into the articulate word of the subject.[37]

It is at this base-level of the art elements that we first encounter our own seemingly miraculous capacity as existing beings to overcome, to transcend the brute given world and, as spontaneous or free agents, transform it into our own kind of substance and into our life-world. It is here that we first exercise the positive power of active *perception,* wherein the world of outward sensations and obscure inner feelings is not merely given as stimulus to some automatically reacting Pavlovian dog, but truly *re-sponded* to (*answered back, accounted for,* as the Latin root indicates). The emergence of the aesthetic elements is the same thing as the emergence of articulate self-transparent *human* perceptual reality, at once subjective and objective; indeed prior to such distinctions. It is *being* which is encountered, wrestled with, conquered, resolved, and wrought into fit possibility for existence, a world of felt and imaged being in which the existent, who is nothing but possibility, can breathe and move. From the perspective of this observation, Croce's assertion that the world in which we have our concrete existence is fundamentally aesthetic rather than scientific is quite correct.[38] No man can live without being able to feel and to imagine existence-in-the-world. Any other world or life can be only an object of the constructive intellectual and practical consciousness

---

[37] *Ibid.,* pp. 206-214.

[38] Croce understands the aesthetic moment or stage in purposing activity as a first and constitutive ingredient in concrete experience. Though my own view remains the same in certain respects, the thoroughgoing existential context in which I place it introduces far-reaching differences.

whose significance and value, in the final analysis, can be found only in its bearing on the world we can actually feel and imagine. From this frame of reference, the real world of our existence is one among a perhaps infinite number of *possible* worlds in which we can feel, imagine, and act. At this rock-bottom base, art and life are one.

The transformation of the brute "given" in sensation into the aesthetic elements marks the point where art and life meet and are quite the same thing. Such elements feed both life and art at their base. Both life and art have to do with possible self-and-its-world. But this first or original element, being in the hands, so to speak, of the spontaneity of existence itself, remains also at its own disposal as something which can serve as basis, either for living out or enacting the possible life-world we call "real," or as material out of which to construct freely and indifferently the possible worlds we call art-objects.

There is nothing to prevent us, in the course of ordinary living, from looking upon our surroundings and the vicissitudes of our life as aesthetic productions. It may even be, as Neitzsche suggested, that this is the only concrete significance life can ever have.[39] That the aesthetic transformation of our experience must stand as the original form which we come to recognize as our own, permeated with the personally known and unknown mode of "being-there," there can be no doubt. But, whether or not out of the original root-elements common to both life and art we can make of life-in-the-world a work of art is doubtful. The spontaneity that we are, cast into the world and abandoned there, is patently not free to be itself in the way that it certainly is in art. The fundamental unchosen, imposed project which is life itself allows for no such freedom. In a world which is forever trying to make you be somebody else, to be nobody-but-yourself is to fight the hardest battle a man is called upon to fight, and never to stop fighting. Though the same at their source, life and art move in different directions insofar as the original elements upon which they are built enter into different kinds of purposing. In art, they are not put together to serve any life purposes whatever; they enter directly into the presentation of free possibilities of being for both self and its world. The aesthetically felt-image of a line, a form, a movement, a sound, can certainly be realized anywhere in the course of ordinary living, but in the explication of life's practical and theoretical projects they seem as

[39] Nietzsche, *The Birth of Tragedy*, p. 42.

intruders that are needed to get our projects started, but which we
have to dispel as we do a daydream if we would go on with our
projects. Intellect and action attend to other things: "futures," to
what can possibly be thought or acted upon. The "Now" of the felt-
imaged world, and of life from which they must start, they neither
confirm nor explore just as it stands. If they are not concerned with
such futures, then they are concerned with "pasts"—with "what
was," or what can be remembered or reconstructed as having been
(concretely speaking, the two are the same).

No doubt some readers will think it incredible that the elements
are the same in art as in the experienced real world. The identity
is best understood when we are able to look upon the parts, the
whole, or even the totality of natural objects in full awareness of
their essential qualities and in complete independence from the
purposes *for* which we ordinarily think things are. To clear his
mind of such purposes, the reader need only look at the unique
grain of a piece of wood, the configuration of a tree, or the shape
and textures of a simple rock, and ask the question as to the purpose of these things, holding back the intrusion of utilitarian, scientific, and theological replies which are apt to suggest themselves
out of force of habit. He will have to admit that the question is
unanswerable, in fact, meaningless. Despite this and because of it,
he will find too that the concrete grasp of what he is observing reveals that perceived lines "take flight," are "playful" or "serious";
that shapes are "foreboding," or "unassuming"; that textures are
"soft" or "hard" in exactly the same way that they are in the work
of art. It is this that explains how it can be that the photographer
with aesthetic sensitivities can achieve such remarkable results by
simply photographing certain objects under certain conditions.
Oriental as well as Western "realistic" painters often work in this
direct way with "nature."

We pick up the elements of the work of art at the point where
we find them and can clearly discern them for what they are in
themselves, considering them not as ingredients of the life-world
of the existent at the very base of which they surely stand, but as
somehow freed from any and all intentionality which would make
any kind of "real" world out of them. In the work of art, they are
made available for the free construction of possible self-and-world
as sheer possible being, indifferently presented—with absolutely
no theoretical or practical strings attached.

The elements which serve as foundation of the life-world (*Lebens-*

welt) are the same ones that, in the art-object, acquire an eman-
cipation of being which permits them to enter into the construction
of any felt-imaged possible world. Neither the demands of reason
nor those of action need any longer determine the way they can be
put together. This is to say that the very same building-blocks
which serve to construct the real life-world are now freed to serve
in the construction of any possible world whatever which can be
actually felt and imagined. A Taoist poet sings

> Heavy falls the rain
> On the hat that I borrowed
> From the scarecrow.

But the feelings and images which go to make up the poem are no
longer quite the same as those which served in real life. The felt-
images no longer refer to the life-world, but to a subjective possibility of feeling and of imagining a possible-self-in-a-world. In the
same way, the characters, the actions, and the setting in *Macbeth*
are no different from those which present themselves in real life,
but they do not now serve any of life's purposes—they are freed
from every practical and theoretical project, as these must explicate
themselves in the world. Movements in the dance accomplish
nothing (one "goes" nowhere in the dance), and are not intended
to accomplish anything, except in and for the presentation itself of
the dance. Certain felt-imaged-sounds in real life can warn us,
soothe us, disturb us, announce events to come; in a musical composition, they continue to function in the same way, but not in and
for the real life-world. To live in the world in which they effectively
function, in fact, one must momentarily cease participating or living
in the real world.[40]

[40] No sooner do we look upon concrete things than we drown them in our projected theories, investing them in our practical concerns regarding use. Thus,
the texture of the rock appears as something made to suit the purposes of the
house-builder, and the cloud formations as something made to satisfy our scientific and theological nomenclatures.

REPETITION, ALTERNATION, HARMONIZATION, COMPLEMENTATION, AND OPPOSITION

From the moment the elements appear in the world of the art-object, their own peculiar kind of interdependent self-discrimination and interrelation also appears. But even in this ordering, in which retention of self-identity and unification with the rest is made possible, they do not necessarily reveal any difference from those which function at the base of life. In the Taoist poem, a hat borrowed from a scarecrow can really be heavier than an ordinary hat, say, placed in a more protected place. The difference lies in the fact that the interrelation of feelings and images is now projected on an ideal plane, where questions of real weight, hats, rain considered as such, no longer have any direct relevance. Real life becomes now only a kind of raw material, a residuum of living which serves to feed and to re-enact spontaneous feeling and imaging as if to begin spontaneous being-self-in-a-world anew and fresh from the start, for the sake only of presenting a certain pure possibility of being. This difference permeates both elements and their orderings when viewed from the standpoint of the whole which they serve, and in which they effectively function.

It is not the fact of the noses and eyes which Picasso displaces, multiplies, or eliminates from the figures in his paintings which make them unlike real life, but the convincing feeling and imagination which they make present. As it is, in real life, the absurd is in evidence, pervasive, all-present enough. In art we come to see it as a convincing possibility whose presence as such raises no questions, precisely because it poses nothing that we must act upon or have to coherently conceptualize. The sculptured image of a griffin or unicorn is "not of this world," and it is precisely because of this that it is aesthetically convincing as a possibility for feeling and for imagining. But the parts out of which it is concocted and the manner of its "put-togetherness" remain intelligible as elements and relations drawn from a world of experience which is relevant to the world of thought and action. The unreality of the art elements and their inter-relations is to be accounted for, therefore, entirely on the basis of the disposition and intentionality of the spontaneous subject—on what he does with his spontaneity. The incredible color combinations which can occur in real life—say, in a sunset—are often thought to be impossible and entirely fabricated when they are "represented" in a painting; the unbelievable absurdities which can occur in the real life of humans appear unbelievable when "represented" on the stage. But in these respects art and life are not basically different. The important thing here is that the art work does not present what is or is not possible in real life: it presents only what is possible as a felt and imagined possibility, regardless of whether we think it possible in life. Art elements are reminiscent of their source, which is the first and original source also of life-in-the-world, and their inter-relations are also reminiscent of the fundamental ways in which the original elements common to both art and life are related.

Let us consider the simple relation of self-identical repetition of any element, be it in life or in the art-object. As felt-image in the art-object, this repetition is the root-relation which unifies, and holds together the whole. In life, too, as Kierkegaard and Nietzsche both clearly understood (though in somewhat different contexts), *repetition* is what holds life together, giving it abidingness, being-ness, or endurance.[41] A painting in which no line, no shape, no color, no size, no direction, no movement, was in any way ever repeated would be complete disorder. (Both in the art work and in life, such absolute unrelatedness is unimaginable, though approximations to it are not). Primitive unity, such as self-identical repetitions of a drumbeat, illustrates perfectly what lies at the base of any unificatory relationship among elements. But this manner of unification has obvious limitations, even if fundamental to any and all ways of unifying elements. If persisted in, it easily degenerates into monotony and boredom, even hypnotic trance, which no longer permits controlled presentation of feeling, but opens instead the flood-gates of the irrational, which is neither recognizable life nor art. Absolute self-identical repetition of any element is really not possible, considering that some interval between the elements repeated is essential for any repetition to occur. A sustained, continuous, and self-identical sound (which would not be true repetition) comes closest to this absolute limit, but after a while

---

[41] In Nietzsche, the existential notion of repetition is expressed primarily in his strange doctrine of Eternal Recurrence; for Kierkegaard's version see Bretall, *Anthology,* pp. 134-152.

it passes out of all notice, neither unifying nor disintegrating experience—city dwellers sleep peacefully in the midst of din. It is for them as if the noise did not exist. True repetition of self-identical elements is possible only because of the presence of some element other than that repeated, be it a pause, a space, a rest—some contrast with whatever surrounds the repeating elements. A single color of the same hue, value, shade, and intensity covering a whole canvas must at least contrast with the mat, the frame, or the surroundings of the picture before it can be noticed as a "sameness" of color, in which case it can serve effectively as background for other elements. True repetition is thus alternate repetition of different elements, both in art and in life.

Alternate repetition gives birth to the elementary *theme, unit,* or *motif,* which can, in turn, become an element that can be repeated in alternation or in any of several other ways. Clusters of alternate repetitions of the same elements can, in turn, become more complex units which can be repeated variously.[42] This, too, is a phenomenon observable in art as well as life.

But repetition by alternation need not be of self-identical elements or clusters of elements merely. It can be by grades, or harmonious variations of the same elements. Though differing, harmonious colors, such as colors which are members of the same family-hue, but differing in value and intensity, constitute an effective diversifying, as well as a unifying agent. In such unities, neither complementary nor contrasting elements are admitted, the explication of the whole being carried out entirely by gradations of the same elements. In art as in life, such unifications are achieved by a minimum of conflict and diversity; everything is in browns, let us say, lines flow into other lines and into the whole, shapes grow out of one another, events flow out of other events. Nothing is abrupt, nothing cries out for integration, for self-surpassing. Such unities may very well be rich in individual themes and motifs, but these blend into one another without true contrast or opposition. In terms of life, such unities are comfortable, safe, familiar, and conducive to restful repose and self-satisfaction. Though in a different way, they too, like self-identical repetition and alternation, skirt boredom and hypnotic self-oblivion. Their weakness is that no real emphasis of single elements is possible by their route.

[42] Thus we can speak of primary themes made up of secondary ones, or side by side with them.

As aesthetic possibility, of course, such harmonious unification of elements carries no necessary approval or condemnation of life so ordered; it only exhibits what it is like as a possibility.

Beyond such alternate harmonious repetition there is a complementary kind of alternation and repetition of elements which enriches repetitions by introducing a new and peculiarly vitalizing contrast. The elements alternated and repeated are here mutually self-completing, inseparable poles of one another. An orange and a blue, when juxtaposed, reinforce one another's intensities on the canvas; a yellow, surrounded by a field of purple, becomes more intensely yellow. But when the orange is mixed in with the blue, or the yellow with the purple, a new hue or color quality is generated. The scale of juxtaposition and blending of complementary elements runs a course which generates the highest intensification of the individual complementary elements, on the one hand, and melts both into the undifferentiated ground, on the other. Complementation as a way of unifying elements can individuate or suffuse them. It denotes a kind of equilibrium which can verge on either disintegrating disunity, or undifferentiated dull unity, in both life and art. Complementary poles stand too ready to use one another for their respective exclusive independence, or else to yield to one another, in varying degrees, in total self-nihilating submission.

Still another sort of arrangement of elements is that of direct conflict and opposition, in which not complements but true opposites enter into repetition and alternation. In life as in art, this is where we find dissonance, clash, suspense, shocking surprise, immanent threat of dissolution of all unity, explosive, climactic crises. Where this kind of relation can be contained within the whole, the very violence in the contrast of elements serves sometimes to generate an even more binding force and power of unification of the whole than any of the others previously mentioned. Alone, it could never stand as any sort of unifying agent. The Greek tragedies are supreme examples of perfectly interwoven repetition, alternation, complementation, and violent discord of elements.

Needless to say, this is only a sketch or general outline of the essential and fundamental ways in which the elements of the art work may come together in the whole presence of the art-object, and how these reflect the fundamental ways of self-unification of the existent himself and his life-world. Any more detailed study will be found incorporated later in the text. It is sufficient here to have indicated what the elements and structures of the art-object considered in its execution are, and that they are the same as those embedded in existence-in-the-world. The endeavor to establish existence as a being is all one, be it in life or in the dream of indifferently realized possibilities of being which is art. In both art and life, the spontaneous being of the existent seeks to establish him and his meaning by repetition, alternation, harmonization, polarization, and opposition; he seeks to accomplish the feat by one, some, or all of these measures, depending on his condition of existence, and on the world into which he is cast and by which he is conditioned. The only difference is that in art the struggle to unify existence-in-the-world is a free struggle, projected on the plane of pure felt-imagined-possibility. The common roots that art has with life help explain its indirect revolutionary power over life.

CHAPTER FOUR

Art & Existence

EXISTENCE AND PURE POSSIBILITY

How is the very being of the existing individual constituted so that art is possible? Conversely, what can art mean in the light of the fact that human existence is as it is? Phenomenological inquiry must establish concrete fact, and existentialist philosophizing must proceed to examine matters of concrete experience, unfettered by the restrictions of any system. In an existentialist-phenomenological aesthetic, we must try to see what we can learn about the condition of man from the art phenomenon, and about the art phenomenon from the existential condition of man.

In the face of life's uncertainties, we say, "Anything is possible!" sometimes with the passion of hope or despair, sometimes with detachment and indifference. The possibilities we refer to are casually more or less well-defined by the limited contexts of our life experience; thus, it may or may not rain tomorrow, war may or may not come, a sick friend may or may not die. Whatever it may be, we are making reference to *something* that seems possible. It is through actual being, then, that we understand possible being.

But there are rare occasions when we experience an overwhelming awareness, not of *things* that are possible, but pure possibility *qua* possibility, nameless and unincorporated. It neither springs from nor is directed at a particular hope or despair in our life experience. We cannot pin it down except to say that what we are feeling is the presence of infinite possibility which is not directed *from, toward,* or *for-the-sake-of* anything.

The possible in this manifestation fills us with apprehensiveness in the encounter; it seems unsafe, threatening, even diabolical. It is like Mephistopheles in Goethe's *Faust,* presenting itself as more primeval than Being itself. It is a nothingness restless with stirring intimations of being, a belabored womb from which being itself is to be cast out. Like one whose foot is slipping off the edge of a precipice, we feel ourselves falling headlong into a void. We draw back, grasping for any handhold we can get seeking refuge and protection in the limits or boundaries of reason.

"Anything is possible" in this sense carries with it the notion that nothing—absolutely nothing—*has* to be, and that everything—absolutely everything—*can* be. The indifferently possible confronts us with something-which-is-nothing, and with nothing-which-is-something. For the first time, perhaps, we have come suddenly to see, to understand, that existing man is his possibilities (he does not merely have possibilities); that existence precedes essence; that man is his own freedom; that man is a self-in-the-making; that man is a being that must make itself in its own absence.[43]

The experience of the nothingness which is the indifferently possible puts both subjective and objective being into question. Like a sudden flood, it inundates everything with unreality, affording us what Schopenhauer called the true mark of philosophic talent; namely, an ability to view everything or everyday reality as a kind of illusion hiding another, totally different kind of reality. Suddenly we come to doubt the cognitive modes of our experience: the law of causation seems suspended; unrestrained, spontaneous being makes its entrance like a Dionysiac god.

Nietzsche discussed the pure possible in terms of the mythological Dionysos and his cult. Nietzsche describes what it is to be transported by ". . . the Dionysiac rapture . . . [the] surging, self-oblivious, all-unifying power . . . which penetrates with joy the whole frame of nature in the powerful approach of spring.

. . . Not only does the bond between man and man come to be forged anew by the magic of the Dionysiac, but nature itself, long alienated and subjected, rises once again to celebrate the reconciliation with her prodigal son, man. The earth offers its gifts voluntarily, and the savage beasts of mountain and desert approach peacefully

[43] A. B. Fallico, *The Quest for Authentic Existence,* pp. 50-78.

. . . the gospel of universal harmony is sounded, each individual becomes, not only reconciled with his fellow, but actually at one with
him—as though the veil of Maya had been torn apart and there re-
mained only shreds floating before the vision of mystical oneness. Man
now expresses himself through song and dance as a member of a
higher community; he has forgotten how to walk, how to speak, and
is on the brink of taking wing as he dances. Each of his gestures be-
tokens enchantment; through him sounds a super-natural power. . . .
He feels himself to be god-like and strides with the same elation and
ecstasy as the gods he has seen in his dreams. . . . The productive
power of the whole universe is now manifest in his transport.[44]

Nietzsche points to a state of being that few existentialists after
him have detected—exhuberant, joyfully creative, and unifying. But
he recognizes also that the unrestrainedly free has another, darker
side which is ego-endangering, demonic, primitive, easily degenerat-
ing into frenzy and madness. But he sees the Dionysiac as necessarily being forever counterbalanced by a restraining, form-giving
force which he calls *Apollonian*. Apollo is the form-giver and the
restorer of wholeness. This "deep sense of the necessity of dream-
experiences," Nietzsche suggests, has its roots in an incompleteness,
even illness, at the base of human existence: "the perfection of
conditions in contrast to our imperfectly understood waking reality,
as well as our profound awareness of nature's healing powers during
the interval of sleep and dream, furnishes a symbolic analogue to
the soothsaying faculty and quite generally to the arts, which make
life possible and worth living." But the image of Apollo "must
incorporate that thin line which the dream image may not cross,
under penalty of becoming pathological, or imposing itself on us
as crass reality . . . ."

Concerning the equilibrium-in-tension of the Dionysiac and the
Apollonian in Greek culture, Nietzsche speaks with special regard
for the Dionysiac element: "Whoever approaches [the Olympian
world and Greek Tragedy] seeking moral elevation, sanctity, loving-
kindness will surely be forced to turn away from them in ill-humored
disappointment. Nothing in them reminds us of asceticism, high
intellect, or duty; we are confronted only with luxuriant, trium-
phant existence which deifies good and evil indifferently." The
category of the indifferently possible is, in a way, central to all of
Nietzsche's desperate philosophizing in the face of nothingness

[44] Nietzsche, *The Birth of Tragedy,* pp. 19-42.

("God is dead! What shall take his place?"). For him, the joyous
total giving of oneself to this dangerous freedom is its own sole
law and necessity. "To the extent that man is artist," he writes,
"he is already delivered from his ego and has become a medium
through which the true Subject celebrates his redemption in illusion." Of this radical self-transcendence, he says: "There are people
who, either from lack of experience or out of sheer stupidity, turn
away from such phenomena, and, strong in the sense of their own
sanity, label them either mockingly or pityingly 'endemic diseases.'
These benighted souls have no idea how cadaverous and ghostly
their sanity appears as the intense throng of Dionysiac revelers sweep
past them."

Reading Nietzsche, one senses his powerful and tortured reach
into the darkest regions of human existence. But one also senses the
infinite pathos and the futility of his effort to stem the onrush of
nihilism in his day. The confidence with which he tries to counter
the pessimism of Schopenhauer savors somewhat of braggadocio
and, in any case, betrays everywhere the ineradicable despair of
existence whence it springs. Nietzsche's "Higher Man," his proposal
for realizing fulfilled being in "Eternal Recurrence," his suggestion
that man himself must become god—all show how well he understood the absence of being at the very heart of human existence.
The measures Nietzsche resorts to are extreme. In this light, his
Dionysianism appears no longer as a surging, overflowing, superabundance, but as a lack and a hungering. His Apollonianism also
seems no longer that which merely restrains the irrepressible rush
of generative powers impressing form upon them, but the pathetic
publication of man's fundamental nothingness, his lack of being.
His account of the aesthetic calls, accordingly, for some revision.

What is human existence like? How does it feel to exist as a
man? This is, of course, not a question which can be asked by anybody, or answered for everybody. The very intentionality of the
question as well as the answer given to it depend unavoidably on
the purpose and interests it is made to serve. One man asks and
answers the question in order to reassure himself of his divine
origins; another, to give vent to his resentment at being alive. One
man answers it as if the question itself could never be the object
of questioning; another, realizing that it can proceed in the frank
admission that both the asking and the answer are in the nature of
confessions, a self-disclosure. In the existentialist position of the
question, one either replies from the utterly sincere posture of the

artist, or else fakes both the asking and the answer. The temptation to deliver an account that will please others so as to put forth a good image of oneself, respecting socially accepted oughts and musts, is strong in all of us. But it is only to the extent that we can divest ourselves of all pretense and of all desire to affect others that we can properly examine this basic assumption in aesthetics as in any other branch of philosophy.

Elsewhere[45] I have offered an extended description of human existence as unformed being (i.e., the pure possible), a summary of which will serve our present purposes. Cast in purely expressive, non-technical language, such appraisals may also help us concretize matters which might otherwise remain abstract.

A man may be studied much like any laboratory guinea pig, or he may look into himself as a freedom. The less he looks into himself as a freedom, and the less he endeavors to be and to act as a freedom, the more he becomes fit to be viewed as a laboratory guinea pig. For things and guinea pigs are predictable in their behavior, and men who lose their way, becoming alienated from themselves, become more and more predictable in the same manner. The mark of the free man is that of the sane and healthy man— he is *unpredictable.* He may, of course, be reliable and trustworthy, but that is another matter. A free man is one who can still *choose* not to function as he "should."

As an observable thing or object, a man also falls within the realm of impersonal facts, apprehensible by the sciences, and by logical thought. But that of man which is impersonal fact does not include the spontaneity, the freedom that he subjectively is. As a subject of physical investigation, he is continuous with the rest of physical nature; and as a subject of rational thought he shows up as a cipher or a function entirely absorbed in a system. Whatever there is or can be seen of a man is *all there,* waiting only to be caught in the nets of some system which will "account" for it. Thus the freedom that is a man cannot enter into any account that is given of him as thing.[46] Freedom is nowhere to be found among the observable objects of this world. The subject-agent is doer, not the thing done, observer, not the thing observed, even when the "thing"

[45] See also P. Koestenbaum, "The Logic of Schopenhauer's Aesthetics," *Revue Internationale de philosophie,* No. 51, 1960, FASC. 1., and *The Quest for Authentic Existence.*

[46] William D. Nietmann, *"Breviter Dicta," A Note on Subjective Truth* (Stockton, California: University of the Pacific Publications in Philosophy, 1960).

done is the doer himself, and the "thing" observed is the observer. The doer-seer remains always unaccomplished and ahead of himself in any such account.

Seen as a freedom, an existing individual is not at all a possibility of being inherent or included in the being of the things of this world, but the being itself of possible being. His concrete existence can in no way be deduced from the being of the world. A freedom thus understood cannot be proved by arguments; it can only be lived or enacted, and attested to in the living or enacting. A "proved" freedom is no freedom at all, since freedom is a premise, not the result of inquiry. What Karl Jaspers says about God can be said equally well about freedom: "Only he who starts from God can seek him; his presence is ascertained existentially." [47]

Though a man can choose himself as the freedom that he is authentically, or else as an unfreedom unauthentically, freedom itself is not a matter of choice. Sartre puts it that we are "condemned to be free." Even to not choose is a choice. Though we may escape from ourselves, we yet initiate the project of our self in the act. Though the choice of unfreedom alienates us from our self, self-alienated existence is yet an existential project. It is only in and through our freedom that we can escape from freedom or be that freedom. [48]

Even as a man is not in his body all he could be, by reason simply of his birth in the world, so also is he not all he could or should be as a man, simply because he exists. The project of his being is a fearfully open project, even if set fatally within limits which are not of his choice: birth, and death. With regard to death, however, though a man has no choice but to die sometime, somehow, sooner or later, he nonetheless has the absolute choice to die at any time. This is to say that, once cast into the world and abandoned there, a man remains absolute arbiter with respect to his fundamental project: he can erase it at any moment. This possibility attests to his freedom more than any other. There are, in any case, two very different species of death for each man: his own, and that of any other. When another dies, the world and its course remain the same; when *he* dies, everything ends for him. [49]

[47] Karl Jaspers, *The Perennial Scope of Philosophy* (New York: Philosophical Library, 1949), p. 32.

[48] The point here is that though we are "condemned" to be the freedom that we are, we nonetheless remain free to accept or to reject ourself as that freedom.

[49] Reference is to Sartre's short story, *The Wall*.

The open project of our personal existence is such that non-being comes into being in two distinct forms: things and states that are not, but ought to be, we yearn to bring into being; things and states that are, but ought not to be, we seek to annihilate. At the very center of this uncertain ontological commerce is suspended our naked being. Here we have to choose and commit ourselves, whether we like it or not, either to being something or to being nothing. We are only a reaching-out into open possibilities of being. It is precisely the basic *indifference* from which our reaching-out stems which constitutes our "dreadful" freedom.[50] Thought and action—the theoretical and the practical—are the fundamental ways we have of mobilizing against our own deep-lying indeterminacy. It is by means of them that we are able to convert indeterminacy into determinate being. But the converting grasp, the taking of possession by thought and action, is ever at the risk of bringing error and guilt into being together with the possibilities which are chosen and acted upon. Besides, both theory and practice can effect their settling work only arbitrarily, in the final analysis, leaving the unformed being which underlies and surrounds them on every side unaffected. No action or system of actions, no thought or system of thoughts can appease the hungering for being which is existence, closing the gap between being and nothingness.

We are such beings as are in doubt in their very being; uncertainty is no mere state of mind with us. Kierkegaard thinks that our strongest faith is not the faith which removes doubt, but the faith which finds its depth and very endurance in the constant presence of doubt.[51] Except by some practiced fraud, nothing in this world can completely fill the void for us, or heal permanently the sickness of our profound restlessness.[52] Our condition of being is such that any and all essences, pre-fabricated models of selfhood, must fall under serious suspicion. They raise the question, "Who wants to cover up man's dreadful freedom, and for what motive?" Our condition of being is also such as to put into question every historical ideal, program, and institutional promise of human happiness which costs the fearful freedom that is a living man. Time itself issues forth from our lack of being, for without a living man

[50] So titled by Prof. Marjorie Grene in her book of this name.

[51] H. J. Blackham, *Six Existentialist Thinkers* (London: Routledge & Kegan Paul Ltd., 1952), p. 15.

[52] "Not until the sky is pulled back like a hide will this misery end, unless God is first known!" (from the Sanskrit) *"Inter faecis et urina nascimur!"* (St. Augustine).

there is neither past nor future in the concrete experiential sense, but only meaningless motion. Past and future, hope and despair, conscience and consciousness mark the presence, not of a being, but of a reaching-out-for-being. Thus we are ontologically dispossessed and homeless. Like victims of partial amnesia, we seek our fulfilled Now of Being in pasts, presents, and futures which forever escape us, and can never contain us whole.

Nature's own peculiar indifference attends our formation and expulsion from the womb: a man may be conceived through negligence, rape, marriage, artificial insemination—"nature" cares not how. Once he has come into existence, the reason and necessity for the occurrence is nowhere to be found. Who would miss a man not born? What would the world be missing without him? No mathematical calculation, no rational argument can give foundation to individual existence. It is such that one can only stare it in the face like an appearance out of nowhere, without reason. A man remains a stranger, estranged from the world, yet inextricably bound with it. An existing individual has no substitutes—he is irreplaceable, unheard of, an intruder into being. He stands alone, in an aloneness which is irremediable. With respect to his existence, he stands as the single witness to a grave event—on his testimony everything depends as if at some amazing trial.[53] The account he gives of himself can be given only through the ambiguity that constitutes him as a being. The possibility of self-deception is for him, not a choice like other choices, but an ineradicable possibility of his being. With him, untruthfulness about himself has the intruding power of the dread to be his own freedom.

In the brief span of life marked implacably by a death sentence even before it begins, a man is alone in the decisions he must make in order to give his being meaning. All his decisions are like jumps off a cliff—only rumors and hearsay give him an idea of where he will land. With every choice, the interminable, unexpected consequences of his choices fall upon him, whether he likes it or not. Every choice entails the realization of some possibility of himself; every realized possibility narrows the range of possibilities he can choose; every choice of a possibility may have eliminated the one possibility he should have chosen if he would live with himself, let alone with others. An existing man has his bridges destroyed behind him; "God made man in his image," says Pico della Mirandola in *De hominis dignitate,*

[53] Franz Kafka, *The Trial.*

combining in him all things, and said to him, "We have given thee no
definite dwelling-place, no particular heritage. All other beings in
creation we have subordinated to definite laws. Thou alone art in
nothing restricted and canst take upon thyself and be what thou wilt.
Thou thyself, according to thy will, shall be thine own masterworker
and sculptor and form thyself by thy liking. Thus thou art free to
descend to the lowest level of the beasts. But thou canst also raise
thyself to the highest spheres of godhead. In thee alone I have scattered the seeds of every action and the germs of every kind of life." *

But he runs a race with inevitable death—a race which he must
lose in any case in the humiliating and pre-ordained reification
which turns him into an inert and maggot-ridden thing that must
be hidden from sight. A man is ready to die as soon as he is born.

We must understand that human existence is not a plenitude,
but a lack of being, with the thrust of spontaneity at its very heart.
If art is to be understood as the work of this same thrust, what
shall we say it accomplishes, and for what purpose? What is it
symptomatic of in the constitution of human existence?

Our consideration of the nature of the art-object has disclosed
that art is the expression of a consciousness which antecedes both
reflective thought and practical action. We saw too that, as such,
this consciousness knows nothing about the distinctions between the
real and the unreal, the logical and the illogical, the useful and
the useless, the good and the bad. In its work, aesthetic consciousness remains supremely indifferent to what from the ordinary standpoint must appear to be life's "real" concerns. Dream-like, this consciousness makes and lives in free possibilities of being, cast in a
kind of actuality which is indifferent to time, space, and even death.
As Croce has said, "Before the work of art, we stand as if in the
very presence of the creation of the world." In the perfect coalescence of feeling with image, the original aesthetic constructivity
accomplishes perfectly what neither waking-state reality nor dream
can accomplish separately—it lends wakeful reality to the dream,
and dream-like liberating spontaneity to wakeful life. In this sense,
the work of art implies that all reality is something that is *made,*
or that the possibility of its free and unrestricted making and un-
making stands prior to any and all of its actual formations so that
none can have ultimacy of being and meaning for the existent. The
very presence of the presence which is art casts a veil of illusion

* *De hominis dignitate.*

over all the hard, fast, and pressing realities, even if only by comparison. Who in the presence of the artist's vision has not felt the realities of ordinary experience fade away like transient and distorted dream images? Who in the seizure of the musical masterpiece has not felt with Schopenhauer the presence of the Will behind reality itself, and the surrounding world as only a representation of it? Who in the presence of a Daumier or a Grosz has not *seen through* the human reality as through the artful pretenses of a deceiver?

Apparently art is something more than the work of thought and of action, as these ordinarily operate to circumscribe, delimit, and make manageable the regions of the unknown and the uncertain in our existence. With the latter, the pure possible cannot be admitted without paralyzing thought and action in their tracks. In theory and in practice we move by set guides and rules which help us to map out beforehand the regions of the possible. Validity and invalidity, truth and error, expediency and inexpediency, good and bad, arise and are identified by the limiting marks of what in them is deemed to be possible or impossible. In comparison, aesthetic possibility appears to have no predeterminable limits at all. The aesthetically impossible is, simply, that which cannot be felt and imagined—but who can say what this must be? The man who stands before a multi-headed Picasso exclaiming "Impossible!" has already clearly felt and seen at least that much. But "impossible to feel and to imagine" is an expression which can serve only other than aesthetic purposes, unless one uses it to mean simply that something which poses as or pretends to be aesthetic vision is not aesthetic vision at all. In its admissible use the expression sets no limits on what is or is not possible to feel and to imagine as such.

How must we think of this excess of being and meaning over theory and action, which the aesthetic delivers? That it could be an over-abundance issuing from some Plotinian "One" is out of the question: as we have seen, existence, out of whose bosom it springs, is nothing like that. Shall we think of it as the work of some kind of effort which parallels the main thrust of spontaneity in the constitution of existential being, a competitor to the reality which arises in and for the theoretical and practical consciousness? Should we say that it is the work of that same central thrust in the act in which it overshoots its theoretical and practical mark out of sheer craving for beingness? But we have seen that art is no competitor of our practical and theoretical life; it sets up no substitute reality for these efforts, it embodies no such claim. If its accomplished, full, and free realizations sometimes put what we call reality into ontological question, this is nothing implicit in the aesthetic effort itself: it is "reality," rather, which betrays its own unconvincingness and unsatisfactoriness in the comparison. And if, finally, we are to think of the aesthetic formation as something born out of need which is in excess of that which moves in the search for the true, the good, and the useful, how shall we explain its peculiar and autonomous character, and its manner of fulfillment?

The aesthetic formation stands as a pre-condition to both knowledge and action in the constitution of existence. It carries its own kind of fulfillment; in its own peculiar way it "completes" the primordial and fundamental act of purposing which underlies both theory and practice, dreaming and waking. It thus stands both at the beginning and at the end. But these matters we must examine separately and carefully.

Let us first note that, in the individual and in any whole culture, the pre-reflective, affective, imaginative is prior to any other form of life. Children and primitive people are all superlative poets.[54] At the same time they are also, quite naturally, dealers in direct "miraculous powers." We might say that they are experts in the "uncaused" or the radically originative, in both their cognitive and volitional being. The child and the primitive are, in this sense, inward participants in the original creation. With them, reality can arise by fiat—out of nothing, and for no antecedent reason, unless it be the pleasure or displeasure of sentient being. Here, one comes upon being which is not yet divided or dismembered into "real" and "unreal," "inner" and "outer," "true" and "untrue," "useful" and "useless," "good" and "bad." These distinctions are themselves affectively, rather than reflectively instituted. Ego itself, in whatever sense it may be present, is something fluid, easily transformed and interchangeable: entities, godlike or demoniacal, easily go in and out of primitives, and children know very well how to become the role they feel like playing. In sum, with children as with primitives, experiential reality is freshly in-the-making, and all present.

Now, it is a grave and dangerous mistake to think that the spontaneous and childlike is something which must be left behind or silenced before a mature man or culture can come properly into being. This spontaneity and nothing else is precisely what becomes

[54] Giambattista Vico, *La Scienze nuova*, Vol. I (Bari: Gius. Laterza e Figli, 1928), pp. 74-116.

and must become the adult man or culture. The child enters constitutively into the composition of the grown man, and in such a way that it remains operative and productive at the very base of the adult activity. Those who are not victims of puritanical habits of thought or of unconscious fraudulence and self-deception know that just as the adult who loses his childlike spontaneity becomes ill and is indeed immature, a culture which loses its original enthusiasms and "barbarism," as Vico would call it, becomes sterile and decadent. Men and cultures lose faith and courage to be when they are depleted of pre-reflective spontaneous energies. This is true even where the reflective and practical dimensions of existence are or appear to be full blown; indeed, rational, technological, and political accretion without parallel support of spontaneous feeling and imagination constitute a monstrosity which, sooner or later, declines.

The aesthetic and spontaneous is prior to the practical and the intellectual; that is to say, is an immanent-pre-condition, feeding the main lifestream of existential activity. It is also and above all operative and present in every moment of our human experiential reality.

Like the eye which does not see itself just because it is that through which vision itself takes place, aesthetic spontaneity is everywhere present but nowhere to be found. It takes a special kind of self-conscious awareness to bring it into view; not necessarily a recondite metaphysical posture or attitude in inquiry, but the aesthetic posture and attitude itself brought to self-consciousness. We all are able to gain this perspective when, in moments of supreme natural disengagement from practical and theoretical concerns, we see and feel both inner and outer reality as a dream-like fabric, emerging and unfolding without effort before our very eyes. If at such moments we ask how it would be if our powers to feel and to imagine were suddenly to be totally withdrawn, we understand immediately that absolutely nothing would remain. It then appears, that the whole character of solidity and of necessity that reality possesses is sustained in being by the act of feeling and making images. We understand that, without some minimal element of feeling and imagery, all thought loses content and substance, and all action, aim.

When, moreover, from this same mood and perspective we bring the feeling and the imagining which underlies everything into clear focus, we can find the generative matrix which is ground and support to all our existential realities. And if, in this moment of disclosure, we consider what exactly it is, or must be, that comes in to lend identifiable shape and structure to this possible-everything-or-nothing—to this active pure possibility—it is clear that *speech* alone effects the extraordinary transformation. The indifferently possible at the base of our existential activity posits its own self-presence in an *utterance* which asserts nothing and demonstrates nothing, but which nonetheless initiates everything by making it possible for us to speak at all.

When we say that the indifferently possible announces or posits its own self-presence, what is announced or posited? The answer is that it is in no sense a "what" but only the locus or "empty place" for any and all "whats." As such, this utterance is also the drawing force for the actualization of all realities. No particular kind of reality is therefore announced, but the absence-and-very-possibility of every kind.

The experiment which brings pure possibility of existence into view requires us to look upon both dreaming and waking as equally either real or unreal. This is not to question our common sense judgments on the matter of waking and dreaming, but only to stand, even if only momentarily, underneath or above every interest upon which our theoretical and practical judgments are founded. Only when this is done can we understand that both waking and dreaming realities arise in the same way, even if they involve processes which come under very different controls. If a productive constructivity is at the base of dreaming, it is no different with waking reality. Both are initially the work of purposing, feeling, and imaging; both can be viewed as utterance of the existing individual—a speech and utterance which is, in the first and original sense, a disclosure of existence to itself.

But living is not dreaming and dreaming is not living. In waking life the freedom or spontaneity that we are must not, at the risk of madness, divert us from the practical and the theoretical, or from the set limits of the possible and the impossible which these modes or attitudes of purposing require and impose. This is what we mean when we say that the state of wakeful existence is one in which the freedom that we are is not free to be itself, except in the individual projects initiated by choice or decision within the state. Wakeful existence is, in this sense, like being condemned to dream a single dream—a dream of death and hope, in fact. But, just as such an obsessive dream can show up, at least in its condensed quality, in some single project of the dreaming consciousness, so also can our basic spontaneity show up in its unrestricted form *qua* dreaming amidst the hard restricted business of living—and, indeed must do so if we are to stay sane. In addition to sleep-dreaming itself, understood as a normal occurrence of life, this can occur also under conditions of withdrawal from what we call reality: it occurs under certain pathological conditions, as well as in art. Art, moreover, is to be understood in two senses: as the constitutive precondition of wakeful experience, and as special project under which the normal and necessary original utterance of our spontaneity is put forth on its own account.

The interesting and, may we say, shocking similarities between the work of the aesthetic consciousness and that of the pathological consciousness have many times been noted, especially with reference to what is called "modern" art. But except for the necessarily slanted or tendentious studies of certain motivation psychologists such as Freud, philosophers have given little attention to this phenomenon. Generally, in fact, the feeling has been that any view of art which somehow relates it in any way to the pathological must be offensive, or tear down one of man's great forms of value.

Etymological derivations often help to clarify ideas and to define significant distinctions. "Pathological" derives from the Greek "pathos," which means *suffering*. Our word "pathetic" derives from the same root. Both pathological and pathetic sound rather strange when used in connection with aesthetic expression generally considered. This is in part, no doubt, due to the prejudice inherent in our Western view of human existence and its various facets, a prejudice according to which dis-ease, discomfiture, and suffering are characteristics, not of the human condition taken as a whole, but only of certain of its vicissitudes. An Oriental Buddhist, or an early Christian might conceivably feel differently.

To us, the observation that art or the aesthetic generally is *pathic* —index and symptom of existence's ontological lack—is important. For although there are many other ways of showing that human existence is a lack rather than a plenitude of being and meaning, none is more evidential than the art phenomenon itself. To this must be added the aspect under which art is not only symptomatic of man's congenital incompleteness of being and ontological need, but also nostalgic in the original sense of the word (*nostos,* meaning a return, and *algos,* meaning pain), homesickness. On the very face of it, the art phenomenon is in the profoundest sense testimony

to the pain deriving from man's homeless condition and his lack
of essence.

PATHOS AND *NOSTOS* IN ART

If we can say that the wakeful dream of art represents a deep
endeavor to "complete" the primordial act of purposing which
underlies existence and is substratum to thought and to action, we
will be better able to understand the nature of the completion.[55] First
we should be able to understand the sense in which this completion
can be no substitute for the practical and theoretical formations of
the work of spontaneity. For, while the products of both theory
and action represent, on the positive side, the realization only of
what is possible according to whatever choice of standards and
principles can be made, those of art present the pure possible as
such, without limitations except those required by existential honesty, or that imposed by the capacity or lack of capacity to function
aesthetically in the first place. (There may be beings that are
ontologically or in their very being absolutely *dumb;* at any rate,
from the standpoint of phenomenological observation, anything
that is a *thing,* rather than a freedom, must be so.) The aesthetic
formation is thus truly an extension of that same spontaneity or
pure possibility which is at the very base of life: it is, more precisely, a limitless self-acceptance of the nothingness which existence
is. It is in the limitless self-acceptance that we must seek for the
deep significance of the pathic and the nostalgic qualities of the
aesthetic vision.

In the theoretical and practical efforts, existential being achieves
a momentary resting-place from which to seek and to find another.
Only physical death can end action as we know it, and the quest
after truth can be closed only by the death of the intellect which,
for being not so visible, is no less final. But despite the fleetingness,
the practical and theoretical search after being is one in which we
of necessity "pretend" a certain kind of finality, lest we feel defeated before we begin. Here, the purposes for which we act and
enact thought must not only be made to stand *before* us before we
start, but present existence by which we seek to gain our purposes,

[55] Plato, Schopenhauer, and Nietzsche among other philosophers were most
aware of this problem.

must be voided of all but instrumental value, and dissolved, or consumed for the sake of a future fulfillment. The projection in thought and action is thus always toward some future, an endless flight from the here and now, and the path traversed to get there entirely annihilated along the endless way. This is a flight, more- over, in which the fundamental character of present existence as open and pure possibility cannot become owned without self-defeat. In order that the ends of action and of theory be served, the im- possible—that which not only is not but cannot be—must be in- stituted somehow to delimit the purely possible. To put it another way, though built on the very foundation of existential freedom without which they could not come into being, theory and practice must, in the very act in which they are explicated, disown free activity. This may explain why the very attempt at an intellectual or logical "proof" of human freedom must necessarily deny what it asserts; the necessitation of logic which must be affirmed in the act stands prior to the freedom which is proved or demonstrated. (The attempt at a "disproof" gets involved in the same dilemma, only in a different way: strictly speaking, a man must be capable of choosing freely in order to prove or to disprove anything—no assertion makes itself by any force of its own, and the force of logic works only on him who has already freely chosen to follow logic.) In sum, although theory and practice, too, come to completions of the existential effort which are in spite of the nothingness which is the purely possible, such completions are not made—indeed, cannot be made—in the absolute and limitless self-acceptance of the act of spontaneity. If we dare, in this connection, to use the word "pretend" even in quotation-marks, it is only to convey the idea that the theoretical and practical efforts are and must be in their own special ways fundamentally *arbitrary*. They are not, how- ever, self-owning of their arbitrariness. Just as no statement can be scientific or rational if frankly prefaced with, "this is the way I want it to be!" so also no action can be realized on the conviction that what is gained by the performance will not immediately or eventually bring some kind of definite solution to our problem. Though they certainly should be the undertakings of free men who own their own freedom, it is clear that serious thinking and effective human action cannot be the result merely of unrestrained, open, and spontaneous purposing.

In contrast, the aesthetic effort proceeds in its work in an entirely different way. Just because spontaneity is here self-accepting and

self-owning its self-completions are not effected in projections beyond itself, but in itself. There is no need here to set prior limits
within which purposing activity must move in explicating itself.
Nor is it the case that pre-existing or pre-established limits are put
aside or forgotten, but rather that none are even suspected. In
theory and in practice we must move between the Scylla of the
possible and the Charybdis of the impossible with suspicion and
caution. But in the aesthetic, our innocence is our armor. In a
profound sense, we want nothing, anticipate nothing, seek for nothing beyond the immediate realization. Above all, we postpone
nothing, so that time no longer escapes out of the now into an un-
reachable future. We make our entrance, our showing in being just
as we stand and, what is more, we somehow are able to make this
count and suffice *convincingly*. Because the purposiveness-in-the-act
is indifferent to the ends of both theory and action, the very completions which we thus effect remain free and immune from every
sense of adequacy or inadequacy, as these might be determined on
rational or practical grounds. The presentations of art are adequate
and fulfilling of themselves without further need to be more "truthful," more "good," or more of anything else. They put nothing to
disadvantage, they expose nothing; they put on exhibit, not a kind
of reality other than that wrought in the work of theory or of
practice, but the act itself which makes any and all kinds of reality,
just as it works in itself.

If in the exhibition the creative act becomes freed and disengaged
from the responsibilities which normally must attend human purposing, if a certain richness and power is in this way clearly attested
to, the fact remains that the aesthetic completion is evidence also
of ontological poverty and destitution. The pathic in art resides in
its announcing a mode of being which needs to *dream* reality.
Like the beggar indulging in fancies of princely opulence, existential being attests to its profound deprivation of being by its aesthetic projections. A being that has being has no need to dream
being. A being that has being, in fact, has no need to make or even
to have any sort of reality: it is fully its own reality. Just as a man
in exuberant full health no longer *has* a body, but *is* his own body
(the sense and feeling of having a body, or the duality and schism of
body and mind derives from aches and pains, or a sense of limitation
and impairment in power-to-enact purpose), so also a being in full
possession of itself has no need of presentations and representations
of any other. The mythical, poetic account that Diotima of Man-

tineia gives of Eros in Plato's *Symposium* expresses perfectly the condition of the being that is human.

Now, in speaking of the aesthetic formation, we have to consider the part that this plays at the base of all experiential reality as well as its own fully disengaged expression in art. The element of the pathic is evident in both. Regarding the first of its expressions, we must necessarily limit our remarks here. How we encounter the indifferently possible at the base of our ordinary experience has already been alluded to. Under the proper attitude and posture, the world presents itself to us with the same surprise, unaccountedness, and spontaneity as the work of art (only those whose eyes are dimmed by cynicism can fail to see it). In the pre-reflective moment of awareness, experiential reality first arises not only as unprecedented and causeless appearance, but also as actualization of sheer possibility without intellectual, utilitarian, or moral limitations. Before a man has time to invest this reality with rational justifications and practical and mnemonic references, it stands before him as something seen for the first time. But with it there comes also a note of distress, a sign that something is lacking. Like him who, awakening from undisturbed slumber, feels the confines of a world in which restrictions are put upon spontaneity, the spectacle before us can also mark the flooding rush of the incomplete, the not-done-and-having-to-be-attended-to. The first appearance of our ordinary experiential reality reminds us of our existence, of our tragic destiny. The first appearance of the world at any moment of existence mirrors our ontological disorientation and the very birth of our questioning and our concern. This is not to deny, of course, that under other, non-philosophical moods and attitudes this same first notice of our reality in its emergence can be the occasion for joyful unself-conscious immersion in the battle of action.[56]

With the aesthetic formation, the pathic in the sense we mean here to refer to is a little more difficult to point out. No small part of the difficulty resides in the fact that art has traditionally come to be associated with beauty. The beautiful, in turn, is associated with whatever pleases and suggests itself as ideal and perfection— an object of desire. Identification of art with the beautiful in this sense has ever been a pervasive error in aesthetics.[57] And this is

---

[56] Such confidence and extroversion, in fact, always attends healthy enthusiastic action.

[57] R. G. Collingwood, *The Principles of Art*, especially pp. 16-104; also B. Croce, *Estetica*, pp. 92-95.

surprising, considering that so much of the great and respected art in every culture has to do, not with the pleasant and the desirable, but with the ugly and the forbidding. Michelangelo's *Pietà* is not beautiful in the sense that it is pleasurable, nor are Picasso's *Guernica* or *Guitarist*. As such, pleasing, desirable, and attractive define the objects and objectives of action, not of aesthetic contemplation. This is not to say that the aesthetic necessarily concerns itself with the unpleasant and the unattractive, of course, but simply that it is utterly indifferent to such categories.

It is not the satisfying or the unsatisfying as such, which show the pathic character of the aesthetic formation, but the real-unreality, or unreal-reality of it. Just as ordinary experiental reality exhibits its pathos by the fact that it is something necessarily to-be-acted-in-and-upon or a reminder of our ontological impotency— the aesthetic presence shows it by the fact that it comes, in its very being, as something which in no sense elicits or refers to action or to practical concerns. But care must be taken at this point not to suppose that the pathos in art resides in that art is escape. Aesthetic purposing moves neither toward, nor away from action or existence, but *in* it. Of course, if one wishes to mean beauty as something other than the sensuously pleasing and the attractive (which is what many philosophers have done) then it is proper to say that art is concerned with the beautiful and that true beauty carries always a note of sadness and pathos.

By its very presence, the aesthetic evidences a profound and frank admission of *defeat* in the existential endeavor to arrive at Being and fulfillment by reflective and practical means alone. Not that the aesthetic is, in Freudian terms, anything like wish-fulfillment, but precisely because it is intended to fulfill no wish at all. Wish-fulfillment is never without the element of shrewd compromise, of adjustment to the practical and theoretical circumstances, while the completions of the aesthetic represent absolutely free formations. The latter are pathetic, not in the way in which a man defeated in the ordinary pursuits of life and crying out his despair can be called pathetic, but as the child is pathetic who, unsuspecting of both defeat and victory, laughs and cries indifferently and to no purpose amidst a world of real or pretended savance, self-assurance, and self-righteousness. It is because there is never in the aesthetic any pretense at knowing and possessing, and that the aesthetic formation is the work of a being so completely destitute of knowledge and possessions in the ontological sense, that art is pathetic.

Again, we do not now refer to the pathetic directly spoken in particular art presentations, but of that which is present in them all. Picasso's *Guernica* or his *Guitarist* give direct utterance to certain concrete and unique feelings of the pathetic in human existence; Dante's *Paradiso,* or even the *Sermon on the Mount* (taken as a great poem, which it certainly also is) are profoundly pathetic in quite a different way. The reach, the aspiration, the longing, is here not only in complete disproportion to the practical and logical realities of our existence, but the complete lack of argument or justification—the desperate gratuitousness of the vision— bespeaks its own special word of pathos. The effort at giving reality to the unreal is, at the theoretical and practical levels, a mark of strength. But this is so only because we proceed in these efforts by the guideposts of what, vaguely or clearly, we feel can or cannot be done. In the aesthetic dimension of our being, rather than having any rules to go by, it is the rules themselves which must be improvised, as if one were confronted not merely with the task of making reality out of nothing but of producing as well the very rules to go by, *and for the first time*. But even more than this, the necessity of having to make the unreal out of the real, and the real out of the unreal, speaks for the infinite pathos of art.

Careful existential evaluation reveals that the art formation is indicative of profound, radical disillusionment, not with respect to any particular outcome of the life of thought and action, but with all possible outcomes. Hence the aesthetic disengagement, and withdrawal from all mediated purposing—from purposing, that is, whose expression requires the dualities "inner-outer," "subject-object," "means-ends," "past-future," "premise-conclusion," together with some mediating term in between. And although the disengagement and disillusionment does not breed substitute or rival realities, it does generate a parallel reality which is the art formation itself. Earlier we noted that, although in time, this parallel reality is not of time; that it resolves duality into unity and immediacy; that it returns the central spontaneity of existence to its own free and unrestricted source. We suggested that in the aesthetic, the original spontaneity of existence returns to free and indifferent reality-making for its own sake. If, with respect to absolute being, the practical and the theoretical realities remain forever unfinished, aesthetic reality, although finished, is *prematurely* so. In this, too, resides its pathos. In his tragedy, man is a being who must dream his answer to the question: Does being have any meaning?

Prematurely, he answers either Yes, No, or Maybe, indifferently. The prematureness is evidenced by the splendid indifference of the answer. Only a god, which man clearly is not, could create reality so indifferently. In its startling arrogation, all art is pathetic.

Thus it is that the formations of art constitute a strange kind of superfluity or excess. Plato saw it as the work of a madness—a divine madness, and he was as profoundly perceptive here as in his view of knowledge as recollection. Further, he drew a connection between the madness and the recollection, which, though quite different from the one we are about to draw next, nonetheless serves us as guide.

If the work of art stands witness to man's lack of being, and to the pathos of his hurried naive attempts to play at possessing being, it likewise reveals a submerged, dreamy memory of what it means really to be—an infinite longing for a plenitude of being somehow once known and owned but now forgotten. But the indefinable remembrance—the *nostalgia* of being— significantly involves no turning back to some temporal past or "has been," even as it involves no prospecting toward some temporal future. The Being that existential being remembers and longs for in aesthetic aspiration is one *in depth* or in a *Now* of the being of spontaneity itself. This, too, is a phenomenon observable and describable like the others.

The state of destitution, and the consequent ontological foolhardiness patent on the very face of the art formation, is not such as to preclude a faint self-remembrance of the existential being as a being who is at-one with the power of being itself. The very pathos of the madness emerges precisely out of the contrast between the lack which is the basic spontaneity, and the peculiar fullness which is indifferently fashioned on this same groundless ground. (The work of art is a fullness resting on freedom alone.) The fullness of being of the work of art resides in its absolute finality—it is a being complete in itself. A possible world realized without even the need of its having to be the best or the worst surely denotes absolute power of being without limit. And although such power is only in dreamful play, as it were, and as such is pathetically indicative of a deficiency in power, we have to account for the model of such a thing. It must be that existential being somehow remembers what it is like really *to be*—to be the power of being itself—else it could not even play at it.

But the reader must not suppose that we are asking him to make inferences merely, or to speculate; these characters of the aesthetic are either experienced, or they are nothing. Existentialist ontology rests on concrete, empirical, psychological fact. To grasp the recollective element in art, one must catch himself, for instance, in the act in which the musical piece, the pictorial vision, the poetic mood are intimately owned like long-lost but now recovered parts of one's own very being. We "knew it all along," or "we could have said the same thing ourselves," or "somehow, somewhere, we heard or saw it before." Careful observation of the underlying phenomenon reveals that the memory in such cases is more like a recollection of oneself, or of a way of being oneself, than it is of some thing or event remembered. It is more like returning home from an alien land. The identification is no ordinary identification such as we experience when we feel with and for a certain character in a novel, or are accepting of what we see and hear because it gives us pleasure. The identification is more like a secret confession to oneself of one's own constitutive role in the enactment of experiential reality. No particular or special kind of feeling or emotion associates with it. More precisely, we do not merely suffer the emotion: we possess the power of its enactment in independence from any and all pressures issuing from what we call real life. In the perfect coalescence of feeling with image and image with feeling, and in the reintegration of both in the pristine act of purposing, we know what the possible feels like because we know ourselves to be its creators. Now, in this, there is a profound memory of the act itself of creation, as if we ourselves were or had once been the creator, or at least present at its first enactment. We despair with Roquentin, suffer loss of will power with Meursault, become blinded by divine light with Dante, experience infinite boredom of being with Mephistopheles—all as final possibilities which complete indifferently the very effort at being at all. But the completion is effected always without ever forgetting the ontological limitation of our true existential state.

Such appropriation of unrestricted power, of the power of being itself, is like a permissible madness. What makes it "legal" is that it comes without intent to act or to be acted upon "really," or, better still, without either lack or presence of such intent. But, except for the memory of the power of being imbedded in this ontological play, all art would be mere diversion, if not silly altogether. As it is, it carries instead an element of seriousness which can only be called *religious* in the profoundest sense of the term.

For, just so long as the creations of art are a reality, all our realities remain tinged with a veil of insubstantiality and provisionality, as if awaiting final approval. Art keeps alive our sense of the omnipotent; it feeds the soul with its profoundest intimations of the divine—of the memory, that is, of Being itself.[58]

Two different senses of the nostos in art can be discerned. The first, just discussed, has to do with a dim memory of the reality-creating act per se; the second, with the memory of what it is like to accomplish the full *deed* of creation, erasing the "waste" of time thereby. Under this latter aspect, the art formation presents us with the completed ontological fact, a sort of consummation of the act of being. Only in the aesthetic do we ever, even remotely, approximate the *completely* made and formed.[59] The work of art is the completed fact in the etymological sense (factum = that which is done). Not until after the creation was God able to see what had come of his act, and to see, also, that it was good. On this analogy, the aesthetic—and that alone—ever gives us the feel of the truly finished or accomplished. Every other mode or kind of reality we know carries the marks of incompleteness, if not of abortion and failure altogether. The easiest phenomenological observation to make is to see that the art work stands before us with a kind of unrelated beingness and finality that no other object ever possesses.

But care must be taken not to confuse this sense and memory of the ontologically accomplished with our ordinary sense and memory of the "has been." In our ordinary memory, being has already faded away into non-being by its acquisition of status and finality; to "have been" is to have become depleted of actuality. In the aesthetic *factum,* the closure and finality of being is achieved, rather, by a compression of all the dimensions of time back into the single dimension of a *now,* in full and complete actuality. We saw earlier that the work of art has neither past nor future references. We might add that the peculiar fixity and settledness of being achieved in what is called "still life" in painting, is a characteristic of all

[58] Surprisingly, theologians have rarely given art its religious due; see Charles W. Kegley, "Paul Tillich on the philosophy of Art" in *J. Aesthetics and Art Criticism,* XIX/2, 1960. Prof. Kegley quotes Tillich as asserting that as far back as the period immediately after the first World War "he came to the conclusion that an apple of Cézanne has more presence of ultimate reality than a picture of Jesus by Hofman."

[59] John Dewey would seem to have this characteristic in mind when, in his *Art and Experience,* he refers to the aesthetic experience as "An experience."

art: in art, everything *is,* nothing is becoming, or has need to become.

Perhaps it is this characteristic of the aesthetic which has ever attracted the mystically oriented philosophical and religious mind. It is art that has provided the experiential model and prototype for all philosophies and religions inwardly moved by a yearning for timeless being, and for cessation of all strife. At any rate, it seems clear that, in its claims for immediate realization, religious and philosophical mysticism at its best rests on aesthetic experience. If we exclude the truth-claim from mystical literature, what remains is indistinguishable from art. In some of the literature, such as the *Vedas* and the *Upanishads,* the aesthetic is even spoken of as a grade or degree of mystical realization. But, apart from the historical inextricability of the aesthetic from the mystical, and vice versa, and the way they have ever re-enforced and supported one another, their very opposition, when this shows itself, speaks for a kind of dialectical inseparability of the two. Religion has ever had its graven images, even if only in the uneliminable form of the spoken name! It is significant that all mystical utterance must affirm itself in denying itself, and deny itself in affirming itself: "The Tao that is spoken is not the Tao," says the Taoist for all the mystics. Nor is it clear (to me at least) why the religious and philosophical mystics have, with very few exceptions, always disclaimed kinship with the artist. It must be either because not enough has been claimed for the cognitive value of the aesthetic, or else too much, or of the wrong kind, for the mystical.

Though vitiated by a philosophical context which left no room for existential being, Hegel's profound insight to the effect that art is the sensuous manifestation of the Absolute was too quickly and easily dismissed by modern aesthetics. So, too, were Schopenhauer's remarkable penetrations into the nature of music. Some thinkers, such as James Mark Baldwin,[60] have even gone so far as to make of the aesthetic the culminating issue of the metaphysical quest. More recent philosophers, such as Whitehead, Dewey, and Croce gave the aesthetic central importance in their general conception of value. But with all this, under the sway of the ubiquitous scientism of the times, contemporary philosophy seems to have all

[60] In my opinion, James Mark Baldwin is an American thinker who has too long been neglected. See J. M. Baldwin, *Thought and Things, or Genetic Logic* (New York: The Macmillan Co., 1906).

but forgotten the religio-ontological implications of the aesthetic.

We concern ourselves only with the unappeasable and lingering nostalgia of being which the aesthetic makes manifest in each and every one of its unique and individual expressions. Just as any Derain still-life seems to stop the very process of concrete reality-making in its track, casting that which is made into an eternal light, so also does the agony of existence find its preservation and supreme dignification in an O'Neill tragedy, or a Camus novel. Nor do the seal of eternity and the dignification depend in any way on whether the "made" reflects a world which is desirable or undesirable, "real" or "unreal," meaningful or meaningless. The completions of art are not according to any of the criteria which might apply to worlds represented (we have already seen that art re-presents nothing); if the idea of "completing" be associated with that of "perfecting," then we might say that it is the *act* and not the fact which in art receives its perfection. But the perfecting is here more in the nature of a "closure," a gained self-sufficiency; if there is sincerity and convincingness, there is everything. Incompleteness itself, as ordinarily judged, can in this way become transmuted into aesthetic completeness. Thus, in a Kafka or Camus novel even the meaningless and the absurd take on a quality of truthfulness, of clarity and of self-sufficiency, which leaves nothing to be desired (except to the mind which cannot free itself of the prejudice that only what serves the ends of theory or practice can have meaning). This is true for every great tragedy: the neutrality of the aesthetic is such, in fact, that what we call the tragic, the comic, the epic, and every other way of a total evaluational perspective, are equally truthful. The rule and very condition for the real is here, simply, its presentability or utterability. This constitutional indifference and neutrality is further evidenced by the fact that all evaluational perspectives easily slip into one another, or paradoxically, may even live compresently under the aesthetic attitude. There is tragedy in *Don Quixote,* even as there is comedy in Dante's *Paradiso;* the magnificent posters of Toulouse-Lautrec are, like Modigliani's portraits, both wholesome and corrupt, lighthearted and grave. The only difference between art and life in this respect is that, in art, the presentation of this profound ambiguity raises no disturbing questions, such as the ridiculousness of a funeral, or the obscenity of a legal execution in a gas chamber very well might in real life. The uneliminable immanence of the necessity to act and to judge

for the sake of action in real life abandons us only in rare moments
of relaxation.

But there are such moments when life in its totality is viewed
as we view the work of art. And it is in such moments that we
divine the same pathos and nostos which deeply underlies both art
and life. We sense then that there is defeat in every victory, irremediable dying in every moment of living, sadness in every joy;
we understand what the wise Buddhist means by *Samsara*—the
circle of suffering and of nothingness, the final insubstantiality of
the world. And like a promise recollected from the very depths of
our uncertain being, there wells up the memory of Being Itself.

In the light of what was said earlier concerning the common,
constituting base of the aesthetic and the experiential realitites
this ontological denouement and recollection of our being should
not surprise us. Nor should we, by aping the self-alienated, scientistic mind, fail to give mood or the affective side of our nature the
serious attention and credence it deserves in philosophy. When
our practical and intellectual attachments are relaxed, and life
recedes from us, coming into clearer perspective like a scene which
comes into better view precisely because we move away from it in
climbing a mountain, the infinite pathos of it, and our sense of
being exiles in its midst make their appearance. But what are
the regret and the remembrance about? By what extraordinary
comparison do we come to them? How explain the possibility,
in this neutral light, of seeing the equal truthfulness of the tragedy,
the comedy, the heroic—the absurdity and the nausea of the whole
of the presentation?

From the side of the total dissatisfaction, nothing less than some
sense of the spirit's own power to create out of itself can explain
it; and, from the side of the infinite longing, nothing less than the
self-remembrance of this same power of being. Like dispossessed,
abdicated kings in exile, we know our condition as mendicant
rulers of the real and the unreal alike. We have "intimations of
immortality." But, above all, the freed standpoint of neutrality
with respect to all *desiderata* places us in such remarkable moments
of contemplation beyond good and evil, truth and falsity, reality
and unreality, as if we were absolute arbiters of creation.

In what sense may this profoundest of our recollections have a
truth-value? Do we remember our origins as in a dream, and, cog-
nizant of our fallen estate, intermingle the unequal disclosures in

a foretaste of the eternal in time? Or should we say that our temporality is, in this dim recollection, made to yield its own peculiar
kind of eternity? [61] Questions concerning time, being, and memory
are often raised by philosophers, but rarely in the existential sense
in which they can be directly addressed to the aesthetic in experience.

ON ART, TIME, AND EXISTENCE:
THE CONTEMPORANEITY OF ART

The temporality of our existence presents itself under many
aspects which have many times been noted and dwelled upon.
Rarely, however, has it been considered under the aspects of *waiting,
postponing, enduring,* and *expecting.* Not since Socrates' death-wait
has this philosophical mood been recaptured.

Heidegger's statement to the effect that we live *toward death*
(i.e., we live to die) is only half the story of the contingency and
transiency of our being. We live also in expectation, waiting for
something which is not death, but the fulfillment of life itself. We
live enduring every *now* for the sake of a future which, like a
mirage, is ever receding from view. The very structure of the time
of our existence is such that, as Sartre has said, we are what we are
not, and are not what we are. Nothing is ever in our grasp; the
now of our existence is like an empty place which serves only as
a fulcrum for the effort of going beyond. With us, "it takes time"
for anything "to last," and "to last" involves "passing away." The
time of our existence consists of a present forever fading and decaying into at best a memory, making way for a future which in
the very nature of the case can never arrive. Even the future, as a
matter of fact, is a sort of prospective memory, as the past is a
retrospective one; our sense of identity requires that we "remember
where we are going," no less than where we have been. When we
are momentarily disoriented or forgetful, we ask, "Where was I
going? What was I to do?" When the two memories between which
our existential now is sandwiched disappear, nothing remains of
us for ourselves. Our now of existence is made endurable by two
specters: the "has been" and the "will be"; in itself, the moment
of time is no abode for our being.

[61] The Zen masters would probably agree with this.

True, we are forever filling, or trying to fill this now with abiding, pleasurable states, and minimizing the painful ones. But all pious and rhetorical protestations notwithstanding, it is also true that even the most joyous of states would become hell itself were it to last forever. What would a living man want to repeat in self-identical, Neitzschean fashion, *forever?* Yet, despite it all, the effort itself of living speaks for some realizable *now* of being that is ever within, ever beyond our reach. We might say that the very meaning of this passing away which somehow stays, or staying which passes away—this time of our existence—yearns to be an accomplished now of being with no past or future needed to give it being. As a matter of historical fact, this precisely is the conclusion of the religious consciousness, East and West, after thirty centuries of anguished search.

The reason for touching on existential time at this point in our discussion, is to show that it is, in its very structure, "aesthetically" oriented; that is to say, oriented toward the actual, the immediate, or the now. For, despite its futuristic bend and escape from the present, action is inherently for, and towards, resting-places, arrivals, consummations. In all its exertions, existential effort reaches out for the intrinsically valued, the immediate, and the directly felt whether it ever achieves them or not. Time thus, "runs" in order that it may "stop," and the very chase must be lived-in, savored in its immediacy to be loved and enjoyed for its own sake. Even if, like Faust, we wager our very souls that activity alone will suffice, that nothing on earth will wrest from us a, "Stay!" the sense and suspicion that the very meaning of time is some timelessness never abandons us. Without some immediate, intrinsically meaningful moment of experience, all action becomes senseless. The model of heaven is the immortalized moment of fulfillment!

The fulfillments are there, even though transient and inconclusive. But their infection with death is not the whole of their defect. The nows of our existence are rarely, also, filled with authentic, spontaneous identity and selfhood. Though embalmed in memory, their dying is, to this extent at least, overcome; their common triviality, banality, and anonymity, however, is a different matter. For the existential burden of loneness, and the dread of being our self —of being freedom itself—naturally drive us into the dubious safety-zones of the impersonal and the herdish, where nothing is ever caused, thought, felt, or determined by me personally, but by a "they," or even a countenanceless "it"—an everybody who is nobody. Our nows, under this dilution, are not our own; our identification with them is as with an article made for other's consumption, a thing of commerce. And those nows which, in desperation, we somehow are able to fashion out of our need for self-identical beingness, more often than not must be perpetrated in secret, like veritable crimes that we must hide from others. What is even worse, our moments of authenticity and spontaneity of being, when and if we ever achieve them, contaminate us with guilt. Life is a grave business: innocence and spontaneity are reserved only for very small children, or for the outcast.

How does all this relate to art? In the first place, if we look upon the time of existence as problematic (which it is), and seek for something even remotely resembling a solution to this problem in our experience, we could do no better than to take a close look at art. Not that art is or can ever be the solution to the problem of existence, but it bears all the earmarks of an ideal and final solution; it offers the most illuminating analogy. It also permits a perspective on life which makes life meaningful without resort to the usual criteria of meaning and unmeaning.

We have already seen how the object of aesthetic awareness stands with respect to time. The timelessness of such object consists in its character as full and complete presence: like Aristotle's God, it is all actuality, having no potentiality in its being. With art, the now is everything. But, as was also pointed out earlier, this is not a now equivalent to the present moment of time, but rather a presence which carries its past and future entirely within itself. Hence, there is no "passing"; passing becomes realized as a permanence, a now. The "has been" and the "will be" of Hamlet have equal presence or actuality with his "is"; the whole of the symphony lives in the presence of the part. We can say that in this way, a sort of Nietzschean "eternal recurrence of all things" is achieved which overcomes time itself by making a self-identical and enduring being out of becoming. Existential repetition finds here its supreme exemplification. Only in art do we find experience which endures, not by substitution and displacement, but by the kind of self-identical re-positing which keeps self-identity in being. Dante forever descends into Hell and ascends to Paradise in exactly the same way, and Don Quixote forever fights windmills. And, what is just as remarkable, such "eternal recurrence of all things" entails no boredom.

All art is contemporaneous in its very nature: it is always *now* by the fact that its being is to be nothing else but presence. Notwithstanding the merely useful fiction of the historical and the antiquarian mind, there is, really, no primitive art or art which belongs to other times. There is no more to the presence which is Botticelli's *Primavera* than can now be re-enacted; the idea held by philosophically naive teachers of art appreciation, to the effect that their students must come to "see" a thing belonging to past cultures would be harmless were it not for the fact that very often the student receives the impression that what he is supposed to "see" has nothing to do with his own capacity to "make present" for and to himself.

But above all, we must consider the characteristic of this stoppage of time in aesthetic repetition, by virtue of which the eternalization in actuality is accomplished without regard to human preferences as to "ought's" and "is's." The fact alone of the very possibility of any world whatsoever suffices to justify its eternalization. An Apollo, or a shrivelled-up herring in a Braque still-life are of equal importance—both worthy of being shown forever as possibilities; the life of Dr. Zhivago is no less significant than that of Agamemnon, that of Lolita no less significant than Beatrice's. Sheer possibility takes on infinite value on its own account.

Art places on exhibit a way of validating existence, however meaningless or meaningful it may be: it holds before us value not in its preferential, enlisted forms, but in its pure possibility. It is for this reason that the aesthetic, as attitude and perspective, makes life itself meaningful and tolerable.

There is more than conversational pleasantry in saying of someone that he has "lost his sense of poetry" about life. We refer to the presence or absence of a pervasive, underlying creativity and hopefulness which has the power to transform the quality of our experience. Cynicism is, in the final analysis, a deep-lying negativity of feeling which colors everything that comes into its sphere, a fountainhead of indiscriminate disbelief and disownment. It contains a sort of a priori element of nihilism, an activity of negation. The opposite of the cynical attitude is one in which there is expectancy and willingness to see, to make, and to own values. In a fundamental sense, the latter has an affinity with the aesthetic attitude, and may, indeed, be one and the same with it. Like the visitor to the art museum to whom nothing shows up in his field of vision if he is not prepared and capable of making for himself what he goes there to find, so also the cynic is by his very attitude barred from seeing what he denies is there. The non-cynic has the childlike expectancy of the artist; he can function aesthetically. It takes an ability to dream and to believe in dreams to believe in the value and reality of life: the extreme objectivist cannot but end up in cynicism and skepticism about life and its worth. Luckily, like Hume, no sensible man ever carries his positivism and objectivism to the extreme. As Hume demonstrated, this approach followed honestly and unflinchingly, finally completes the circle back to utter and untenable subjectivism.

But the ability to view life through aesthetic eyes casts it in a special kind of meaningfulness. This is not the meaningfulness which derives from the sight of coherent, logical orderings, nor from the promise of attaining the ends of practical purpose. Rather, it is the kind which derives from disengagement and detachment or from an ability to make life with all its "slings and arrows" innocuous, as something no longer happening, but remembered *now* as in a dream, a dream that is unmistakably *ours*. The element of ownership, of appropriation, is all-important. Important, also, is the paradox that the greatest ownership and appropriation is made possible by the disengagement and detachment. A sense of distance and removal from all urgencies and exigencies seems, in this case, to make possible a more intimate kind of identification than any realizable under ego-centered action. We look upon our life as upon an accomplished work—tragedy, comedy, or anything else it may feel like. Crowned and dignified by identifiable form, life thus discloses itself to us *sub specie aeternitatis,* as the philosophers say, but from a perfectly human existential standpoint nonetheless.

The ability to keep touch with this aesthetic appreciation and resolution of life's meaning is particularly strong with certain peoples and cultures; among others it is much less in evidence. Also, the processes of technological civilization seem more and more to destroy this ability. The "mass man" of modern industrialized societies tends to be not only philosophically bankrupt, but also bereft of the ability to transform life into art. Two extremes of humanity still know something of this aesthetic thaumaturgy: the illiterate peasant not yet spoiled by civilization, and the beatnik born of our decaying modern cities. They still know how to dramatize life into some kind of meaning.

But it must not be thought that the dramatization of life in this sense is histrionic—"being dramatic." There is no pose or pretense, but only the same directness and sincerity which characterizes the aesthetic generally. The ordinary as well as the extraordinary, the trivial as well as the important, the joyous as well as the tragic—all take on a cosmic afflatus, a depth of meaning which lifts them out of the accidental and the mechanically impersonal. The aesthetic dramatization of life hides a deep-rooted will to resist the nihilism which stealthily destroys the very soul of modern man. Against the view which makes of living and of the vicissitudes of living a rat-maze statistic, it forces a personal, superpurposive human significance on life. Under its spell even death and defeat take on heroic and epic proportions, which justify and dignify them. The trivial, the senseless, the absurd become luminous and horizon-filling in themselves. In the same way that the single line, the dab of color, the simple sound become in art the center of a world of transparent meaning, the least event of human living becomes soul-filled and tremendous. The aesthetic attitude is the arch-enemy of the impersonal, the levelling, the non-purposive.

It is also and above all, the arch-enemy of all fakery and phoniness in life. Against mere quantity, it pits quality; against unbounded optimism it pits courageous pessimism; against self-pitying pessimism it pits healthy laughter; and against self-righteousness, deflating contempt. Thus the aesthetic is uncommitted in its very nature, and by so much is equally friendly and open to every possible honest commitment.

It bears repetition that art can have this substantial effect on real life only insofar as the stance at its core becomes extended to living itself in a natural, effortless way. In its honest, virile form, the aesthetic transformation of life is never a superimposition, a thing pasted on to living, but something operative in the very nerve and current of it. Aestheticism, like scientism and philosophism, is a form of fakery.[62]

In relation to existential time, the transformation in question has the same now-realizing effect as art proper. It permits us to see life steadily and to see it whole: it puts life before us, and not just around us. Cast in a timeless light, events assume the same quality as art presences—they acquire the stamp of Cosmic Necessitation. Small or large, fleeting or lasting, insignificant or not, life events all become memorable in a way that establishes their "having

---

[62] "Philosophism," along with "theologism," are taken from Croce, who had the strongest aversion to the modern subservience of philosophers, no less than to what he sometimes called "professorial" philosophizing.

been" on a solid ontological foundation, as matters worthy of being inscribed on the scroll of the heavens. Though in a context which lacks, in my opinion, existential cogency and emphasis, John Dewey speaks aptly of this elevation of experience above the heat and tumult of action as the "celebration of experience." But the celebration is not one at the end of the day's work, not one necessarily marking the "resolved problem," the moment of rest between strenuous exertions. It also can celebrate defeat, madness, even death itself. Commemorative glow comes upon concrete experience, whatever its ordinary import, which fills up time, flooding the world with unique, personal meaning. This is the mood under which we feel that the moment of love, for example, *could* yield the whole meaning of life, beyond which there can be only the living memory of what was. This is the mood also under which the moment of living becomes "unutterable" in the ordinary ways of speech, on account of its unbearable and overflowing richness of subjective meaning. By this magic, the timeless is felt and made present *in* time, lifting the leaden incubus of absolute silence which envelops existence. For, although unutterable in the ordinary ways of human speech, the plenitude of meaning thus germinated *is* the *Original Utterance*—the *first word*.

Just as the aesthetic phenomenon speaks for the root-spontaneity that is the existent in man's very being, so the aesthetic perspective, when extended to life itself in the living of it, lends it the quality of absoluteness. But it is an absoluteness associated with no particular project of the kinds which engage practical and theoretical purposing, as we have seen. There is here no *forced* determination of life's meaning, but, in a sense, a withdrawal from all projects, so that a return to the original font of purposing as such can be enacted. It then appears that life's own hard and alien reality suddenly is returned to its free source of origin. The raw world of fact takes on the quality of a free projection of ingenuous purposing—a pure possibility of self-and-its-world, like the one that art actually is. The ground and very act-in-act of self-transcendence makes thus its visible appearance. The dispersion, the self-nihilating thing that is time practically and reflectively considered, becomes re-collected into a unity; its depleting power, its tearing away at both ends from a center and into nothingness, miraculously ceases. From consisting of a past which by its very nature is no more, and a future which by definition can never be, it is made into a now—a ground for existence to stand on. The existent is freed from having to live between a memorial sepulchre, and a chase after impossible futures and ephemeral dreams forever out of reach. That same now which usually is, as Thoreau put it, "a place of quiet desperation," or a secret place for self-torture or self-oblivion, becomes the very locus of being, the place where spontaneity takes its stand against nothingness. Against the dispersion, the emptying, and the endless nullification of the time of living, the aesthetic stance is able in this way to establish meaningful and exuberant being *in time* by creating presence of being now, and not yesterday, or tomorrow, or never. It has the power to re-compress the dimensions of ordinary time back to their original and primordial source—the now of spontaneity itself. Thus the possibility (even if only *qua* possibility) is realized of our being able to choose our self and our world forever in the same way, in a now which includes its whole past and its whole future within itself

The reason for our insistence on the value and importance of this extension of the aesthetic to life itself must now be evident. For although the aesthetic transformation of life offers nothing on which the practical or theoretical consciousness can actually depend, it is a remarkable fact that, under normal circumstances at least, it is not only allowed but welcomed in the midst of life's hard-boiled concerns. This would not be surprising if the aesthetic were mere amusement or diversion. But it carries, in its own peculiar way, the devastating disclosure that, finally, being can have no other meaning than that which freedom or spontaneity honestly can make out of nothing. Our capacity to look upon life through aesthetic eyes is the same as our capacity to own life in self-recognition, as something wholly ours and of our own doing. This posture re-unites and makes us one with the spontaneity which works at the base of the will and of thought, no less than at the very base of perception. We have to understand that aesthetic realization is not merely a fictitious way of actualizing experience, but rather the fountainhead of all actualness. Without *presence* in feeling and imagination, there can be no actuality of being of any kind for a living person.

Perhaps we can now say without risk of being misunderstood that the art formation, in the last analysis, is not the most important thing about art. More important is the existent's capacity to create value absolutely, of which the aesthetic is the prototype-act. This is particularly true of the form of value indicated by the word "real."

We ought never to use the word real without a reservation "to such-and-such a being," "for such-and-such a purpose." Nothing can ever be just "real" to no one in particular and for no particular purpose. Things are always real *for*, in the light of some purpose, to some purposing being. When a man says of anything that it is real, the questions to ask are, "For whom?" "What for?" The history of philosophy is replete with fantastic claims about What is Real to nobody and for no purpose or, what amounts to the same thing, to everybody for all purposes. In very large part, the endless and inconclusive wrangle, which passes for the history of metaphysical thought consists of little more than such assertions and counter assertions concerning agentless and purposeless "Reals." The fact of the matter is that mathematical abstractions are real to the mathematician for the purposes of his art in the same way that viruses are real to the microbiologist and protons to the physicist for their respective efforts. This is the same as that hallucinations are "real" to the man suffering from hallucinations (the psychologist has to know and accept this reality if he would help such a man), or dream-things to the dreamer. The significant and useful distinction here is not that an abstract reality is disconnected from all agency and all purpose, but that the condition of the agent and the purpose or purposes for which the honorific stamp of reality is tacked onto experience. The quality of reality is, in this sense, a derivative quality. To say this is not to question the worth or usefulness of considering hallucinations to be "unreal" as measured against the perceptions had under more normal circumstances by normal people, but only to say that "real" and "unreal" refer to qualities which come to invest our experience because of who we are and of what we want. The materialist and the idealist can be understood finally as kinds of men holding certain kinds of dedications and commitments. When a man comes forth to propose "ultimate truths" about "reality," he makes very personal and interested proposals, whether he realizes it or not. What justifies such proposals, in the final analysis, is not some compelling objective criterion, but such sincerity as may be there.[63]

The real, then, is that to which we attend, and that which en-

[63] The emphasis placed on concreteness should caution the reader that this is not the usual positivistic view of metaphysical statements.

gages us with others. It involves always an element of selection—
choice. Still and all, over and beyond this, when we view the
matter from the standpoint of the concrete, the element of *actuality*
is what lends any real its transparency, its clarity, its focus in
immediacy. We mean here to make full use of the etymological
sense of the term "actual" (*actus*), so that our reference is to the
aspect under which experience is *enacted* before our very eyes, as
it were. Where this element of enactment is missing, everything
seems to be missing. This is not to say that actuality and immediacy
constitute the determinant of every practical and theoretical reality
in the same way, but only that the nearness or removal of experience from this self-disclosing center gives it the degree of truly
lived convincingness it can possibly possess. Realities which are
distant from this point are at least dim and indefinite; and even
with respect to the most "certain" rational and logical demon-
strations within our grasp, we somehow always seem to await their
further translation into terms of actuality in order to accept them
fully.

Our purpose here is to pick up the special thread which ties
the question of reality and actuality to the aesthetic problem.
Actuality, in the sense first indicated, is the same wherever we encounter it; but in art, as under the aesthetic attitude generally,
we find it in it's pure form, or in its very origination. The aesthetic
is the *presence-making* element in all experience. Hence, too, it
represents the moment of *truthfulness par excellence,* as well as
what we here call *first or original utterance.*

We have spoken of the aesthetic enactment as a purposiveness-
without-purpose, the paragon of sincerity. By this and similar expressions we hope to convey the idea of a pre-reflective directness,
a guilelessness and candor which is possible only when purposing
activity reaches for nothing outside or beyond itself, yet projects
itself irresistably into self-transparent form. The fact that we are
speaking, not of any mechanical process externally describable, but
of purposing activity, calls for a personal kind of characterization
such as is indicated by the word "truthful." We say that art and
aesthetic purposing generally are truthful, not because they adhere
to, or are able to bring into view the truth *about* anything, but
precisely because they dare to show purposing activity naked and
divested of all pre-made "truths." Their very dispossession of all
pre-established truths is itself nothing deliberate or calculated.
"Truthfulness" here refers to the quality of the purposing itself,

not to any judgment which can be made of what it discloses or reveals. Just as the truth ("the way things really are") is irrelevant to the truthfulness of the child revealing himself with absolute candor, so also all preconceived truth according to any and all criteria is irrelevant to aesthetic truthfulness. Right representation or misrepresentation simply do not enter in any way or form. The "untruthful" art work, or the "untruthful" aesthetic view of life do not lie about something that is truly or really other than as represented; they represent, rather, the work of what Collingwood so aptly calls the "corrupt consciousness." [64] Their fraudulence is in their repressing, covering up, or disowning honest feeling, not in their saying something which is not true. Lying in the proper sense of the word is a matter of practical purposing by which things are made to appear what they are not, so that certain ends may be gained. Incidentally, there can be no lying in theoretical purposing, strictly speaking: philosophers and scientists never lie, they only *make mistakes,* which is not to say, however, that they may not be lying their heads off aesthetically in the feeling which necessarily must be at the base of their thinking. This is one of the peculiarities of the objective truth-quest which is rarely mentioned by philosophers. Paradoxically, truthfulness in the sense we are discussing it is no requirement in objective truth-asserting: how one feels or does not feel about what he asserts to be the case is completely irrelevant to the tenability of the assertion.[65]

Jaspers makes the interesting point that it was no loss of honor or respectability for Galileo to have recanted before the Tribunal of the Inquisition, whereas it was quite necessary for Giordano Bruno to be burned at the stake for his beliefs. Truthness would have added nothing to Galileo's objective truths: the earth either does or does not move around the sun; Jupiter either does or does not have moons going around it. Galileo did not have to stand witness to these things, they speak for themselves. That was not the case with Giordano Bruno, for what he uttered he had entirely to own and to back with his life. After all, what telescope could reveal that being was infinite in the way Bruno meant it? His metaphysical proposals, his belief in a God immanent in the universe were not mere discriptions whose truth or falsity could be established independently of his passionate dedication and commitment.

Under the aesthetic posture of our being, we are what we say

[64] Collingwood, *The Principles of Art*, p. 283.
[65] See also A. B. Fallico, *The Quest for Authentic Existence,* pp. 7-49.

and we say what we are—we are existentially what we say, precisely because we are able to say it, and we are able to say it because we are it. No shielding profession, no sanctioning institution stands behind us with pontifical, impersonal authority to protect us. We expose our very souls when we speak, precisely because what we say makes a claim for truthfulness as such, and not for truth about anything.

What kind of truth about sunflowers can one find in Van Gogh's sunflowers? Is it a botanical truth? What may one learn about apples from a Cézanne still-life? In what sense are Shakespeare or Dostoevsky reliable purveyors of "truth" about the human psyche?

To approach Van Gogh's sunflowers with intent to find botanical "truths" or "untruths" of any kind dispels their aesthetic actuality, barring us altogether from the aesthetic presence. They are something that we either are able to enact in feeling and imagination without seeking for anything—unpremeditatingly—or miss altogether. Not the truth about anything, but *the act of seeing itself* is what we take hold of or recover, as if we were seeing for the first time. And it is precisely because of this "firstness," this originality in the act of notice, that we are not permitted even to say that Van Gogh's sunflowers are *not* the truth about sunflowers, for if Van Gogh's sunflowers were in any way intended to represent something, then they could also misrepresent it. Just so long as they are themselves original presence, the very possibility of their representing or misrepresenting anything is out of the question. And here we come to a most difficult observation to talk about.

Actuality or presence which is so freed, so independent, is also absolutely neutral with respect to any justification of its being, except that which derives from the need or the striving which spontaneity itself represents in its most personal form. This means that if we were to ask about the *why* of this way of "making real" called "Van Gogh's sunflowers," the only possible answer would be something like: "Because Van Gogh expresses it, or was able to do it"—very different from "Because Van Gogh thinks so, or wishes so." The point here is twofold: Van Gogh's wishes and persuasive powers have nothing to do with the convincingness of his sunflowers, but they have everything to do with a very unique way of being honestly or sincerely *personal* about seeing anything at all. What counts about this sort of actualization, in short, is that purposing achieves thereby and in the very act, personal, identifiable form. It is not that we feel sympathetic, tender, or friendly toward

Van Gogh and his way of seeing sunflowers, but that the sunflowers, insofar as we can actualize them for our own personal self, disclose to us what it is to re-possess ourselves in the freedom that we are, in relation to a world which shares with us the ineradicable ambiguity of not being what it is, and being what it is not. Where nothing is settled, the only thing that settles anything is a sincerity of purpose that can instate the sense of being *in concreto*. The concrete, to be sure, forever calls for knowledge of a world which is not, in itself, resolvable into the spontaneity of our own being, but this same aesthetic resolution of the duality is also presupposed as very condition to any and all senses of the concrete. "Objective truth" about anything and everything, in the end, awaits the disclosure of what can be personally enacted as actual, like Van Gogh's sunflowers.

What does the truth mean to me, if I cannot have personal beingness therein, or if it can never issue forth into identity-giving actuality for myself and my world? Are not all "truths" of the anonymous and dumb sort like vague rumors about actualities which are supposed to be ever around, but never shown? Is it not actualness and immediacy which finally gives the stamp of personal confirmation to any truth? But, above all, what is a truth to which truthfulness itself is irrelevant?

If we are to say that aesthetic actuality is actuality in its more eminent form, we must add that it is also the whole or the finished form of it, so that it stands both at the beginning and the end of existential effort and existential time. Both the first revelation and the last timeless presence of the actual are essentially aesthetic. Like every civilization, every personal life runs from the sincerity of childlike vision, or the Homeric utterance, to the biographical account or the artistic record which casts human effort into felt and imagined timelessness. Between this beginning and this end, the actuality of the world and of our own being is, except in moments of aesthetic awakening and awareness, only a shifting and uncertain foothold on the edge of utter silence and darkness. The artist in all of us is he who first and finally tells the personal truth about being. He tells how it is possible to feel and to imagine being, and how it felt and what it was like to imagine after it is all over.

To identify aesthetic actuality with the act-in-act of all actualization, and this, in turn, with the personal appropriation which is the essence of truthfulness or sincerity, is to point to a fundamental articulation or *speech* which is conditional to, and constitutive of our essential humanity, and is not just another function or enterprise.

ART AS FIRST UTTERANCE

Although words such as "real" and "unreal," "reality" and "unreality" are honorific words, hiding purposes already undertaken or existential projects already chosen, they can take on an entirely different sense when we focus attention on the peculiarly aesthetic character of the actual. It then begins to make sense to say that we may not only *describe* or speak *about* the real, but also *utter* it. We can even say that, before we can describe the real, we *have to be able to utter it.* The distinction between description of and utterance of the real is a crucial one for aesthetics and for philosophy generally.

One must be speaking before he can speak *about.* The converse, however, is not necessarily true: we do not have to speak *about* anything in order to speak. Those who act as if they hold a man either says something *about,* or can say nothing at all, usually have tenacious dogmas concerning some "Reality." It is false to say (1) that only what can be said in "ordinary" language is meaningful; and that (2) only that language is meaningful which refers finally to what can be confirmed by sense experience or by logical process. The grievous error here resides in the fact that language itself is completely disregarded in favor of scientistic prejudices and linguistic-cultural provincialisms that rarely come out in the open.

It takes no more than acquaintance with children, or some knowledge of another language, to understand that human language is the *matrix* of meaning, and not something consisting of meanings. The symbolic use or adaptation of language is so far from being language itself that it could just as well be called a super-addition to language proper. Children invent language all the time. What cannot be uttered in one language can be said with the utmost clarity in another. What cannot be said in prose can be said in poetry; what cannot be said in painting is said in music, and so on. Some of the most important things that are ever said are conveyed by silence (which is speech of a kind). In short, the whole idea that human speech has certain limits, beyond which men can only babble senselessly, has no justification other than that the person who proposes it has a particular axe to grind about "meaning," especially of such abstractions as "Good," "True," and "Real." (It is an interesting phenomenon of our time that such extreme claims are put forth by men opposing the traditional metaphysicians who, if not explicitly in some doctrine about language, implicitly in their other assertions were guilty of the same error.)[66] Strictly speaking, it is not possible to speak and yet to say nothing. "To say nothing" in any significant sense of the expression, is a most involved and special linguistic project. In order to "say nothing," a man must say a lot!

In classes in semantics, I often invite students to try to "say nothing." Those who take the bait usually do one of three things: make what we call "meaningless" sounds; "double-talk," or make sounds which "feel" as if they should be recognizable words but are not; or remain silent, literally saying nothing. The students are then told that they were, indeed, very articulate about saying nothing—*said it very well*. It's all semantic legerdemain, to be sure, but it teaches the simple lesson that any claim to the effect that language is "saying nothing" is at least ambiguous. Human language must be a deliberate, conscious, and even a "self-conscious" act in a certain fundamental sense. When we speak, we at least always *do* something, even if it consists in "saying nothing." It follows that every case of finding that which is being said "meaningless" is a case of objection to what we find is being done, which happens not to coincide with what we ourselves are doing and expected to find. The very sense of the objection rests on our implicit acknowledgment of what is being done, which we feel should not be done (how else could we object?). It is not that what we hear makes no sense, but that it makes too much sense of a kind for which we have no feeling. When we are disposed to make explicit our own

---

[66] References are to what is currently called language analysis, claiming Wittgenstein as its intellectual father. Wittgenstein's work savors strongly of positivism, though one can easily find in it also pragmatic, mystical, and even existentialist elements. On the surface, it resembles a kind of phenomenological approach to language, but one soon discovers that the behavioristic method predominates. What is most confusing about this interesting writer is that he seems everywhere to be developing some kind of philosophy of language, but, everywhere, also, he is constantly reminding the reader that this very thing cannot be done. Thus, it appears that, like the mystics, he writes much about what he himself asserts cannot be spoken, and, in this, he much resembles the Eastern Yogins who hold that their procedures are like a ladder which one must discard after using it as entirely meaningless. See, Ernest Gellner, *Words and Things* (Beacon Hill: Beacon Press, 1960).

purpose for the rejection—to confess our own project, in other words—the rejection can be useful, as when we say to another, "I see how you feel, but I am now involved with other kinds of feeling." Normally, this should disengage the effort at conversation in an amicable way. As for any sort of serious dialogue or constructive argumentation, the first requirement is that the persons involved begin by agreeing to "do" the same thing, or by attending to one and the same interest or project. It is then that, "You cannot say such and such!" or, "That makes no sense," and similar expressions, have their full justification. There can be neither agreement nor disagreement; neither truth nor falsity where men under the pose of verbal exchange and argument are attending to radically different sorts of projects in interest and feeling. When argumentation, under these circumstances, becomes protracted and progressively more heated, as often happens even among scholars, the participants use one another as sparring-partners for other than philosophical ends.

We cannot leave this subject without saying a word about another serious misconception plaguing contemporary philosophy. There is current among certain specialistic inquirers an almost pathological compulsion to be absolutely precise about words. "What do you mean?" seems, with these philosophers, to constitute the whole of the philosophical dialogue; what is more, the question is not asked with the Socratic intent of defining terms for the purpose of getting on with inquiry on a subject, but simply to kill dialogue by exposing one's opponent's speech as babbling nonsense. Such compulsion to precision—necessary and laudable in certain highly abstract scientific undertakings where language must be stiffened into connotation-less symbol if not into sign—becomes positively destructive in any quest for insight into concreteness. The first thing the philosopher confronting concrete realities learns is that the world is never in accordance with the niceties of logic, never neatly packageable into someone's particular language. Hundreds of thousands of distinguishable sounds and color-tones remain unnamed in any language; except by arbitrary determinations, it is impossible for any man to say precisely when *now* is; no notion of physical bodies ever exactly describes geometrical figures; nobody can say exactly where one's head ends and the rest of his body begins, and so on. What we should say is not that language should have the same kind of precision that serves its purposes in scientific endeavors, but that there are many different kinds of precision, each suited to its own purpose. The poet, the non-analytic philosopher, are not un-precise, they are precise for what they are doing. Anybody who objects really is rejecting what the others are doing, and nothing else.

What we call metaphor is not simply one of the many uses of language: it is the very essence of it. It takes no great etymological knowledge to see that every word in every language is a metaphor, near or far from its original full sense. Even scientific words such as "force" and "motion" are metaphors expunged of their connotative meanings, and mathematical signs are symbols entirely cleared of connotative meaning.

Our use of such words as "feeling," "interest," and "project" suggests much of the kind of "doing" that language is in itself, apart from any extension of it to other uses. But before we speak of this, we had better remind ourselves that here, as everywhere else, obviousness conceals. Just to look at language as we are now doing is difficult. With most of us, language is the sort of thing which is so constantly put to the service of practical and theoretical projects that we come quite naturally to mistake its merely instrumental uses for the whole of it. Somebody said that poets make language, and that everybody else then busies himself slaying it, and to rearrange the pieces for other convenient uses. We succeed so well in assigning to the poet the function of mere entertainer that his presence and work in our midst leaves our misconceptions about language untouched. What we have to recapture is the original revelatory character of the linguistic act in the naked role in which purposing activity itself becomes self-transparent and self-possessed. To do this, we have to put aside the whole notion that what the lexicographer, the grammarian, and every other "language" specialist has to offer has to do with the living act of language.[67] The relation between the concrete activity and the *product* of language is as between a living man and a cadaver. As a matter of fact, the moment we leave the concrete activity of language, we are in regions where "language" no longer "speaks" but must be spoken for; that is to say, it is no longer the kind of doing which is utterance itself, but some other doing or doings whose detection and identification requires much more than grammatical and logical analysis. This is why, in the case of so much philosophical writing it helps not a whit to ask, "What is the man saying?" To ask, "What is he doing?" may get us somewhere. The notion that any-

[67] R. G. Collingwood, *The Principles of Art*, pp. 225-285; also, Croce, *Estetica*, pp. 153-166.

body who *uses* words and their arrangements must be speaking, or even wanting to speak is a pervasive delusion, especially among scholars. No matter how strange this may sound, the fact is that only the poet *really speaks* and *wants to speak* with language. We will see later how it is that the poet, too, needs to help himself with the dead remains salvaged out of the living activity of language, and just what the connection is between these instruments and his own living utterance.

As first and living utterance, the linguistic act is project, interest, and feeling or emotion all in one. To put this in the active sense, we might make use of the Latin derivations of the terms: the first utterance is a whole of pro-jecting, *pro-iettare,* or "throwing ahead," *inter-esse* or "getting inside being" so that "it matters," and *ex-movere* or "moving outside." Original utterance is thus a full program of purposing. It is the undivided matrix of activity. It contains the initial pattern of feeling, action, and enhanced being such that in any single utterance a complete purposive world can be uncovered. When we say of the simplest human gesture under certain conditions that "it told the whole story," this is what we seem to be realizing. Paul Klee's *The Mask of Fear* tells the whole story in an absolutely simple and direct way. The whole story is an actual realization of a possibility of feeling, of interest, and of action which is inexhaustible. Taken at the point of pure and un-adulterated speech, the possibility is actualized or realized *qua* possibility only if it comes coincidentally with any intent to act upon it. Whatever it comes attached to, or with, by way of any enactment other than the actualization for its own sake is not, strictly speaking, the kind of purposing that is language. This is what we mean when we say that before one can speak about any-thing one must be able just to speak ("just to speak" does not here refer to motions in the throat, or the making of noises merely).

Any and all acts of speech are, as such, full and accomplished in their initial, aesthetic form. The fact that we speak in order to get things done—give commands, produce or incite certain reactions, put general concepts in certain orders, whatever—does not change this. The question, "What is speech for, other than (to speak about)?" is a good one, but not for the purpose of uncovering what kind of "doing" speaking itself is. The usefulness of looking at speech as a kind of conveyor-belt or machine which transports feelings, ideas, and the like from one place to another is naive in the extreme when we construe it as revealing the very essence of speech.

For, when this is done, the cart is put before the horse, and in the following way.

We ordinarily assume that language is best studied by describing the "facts" of it, organizing our descriptions into some kind of order or system, and then, perhaps, generalizing for purposes of prediction. Our model for the "data" is, as with every scientific inquiry, that of observable, objective "fact." In the case of human speech, this can only be either *behavior* (some externally observed occurrence or series of motions), or elaborate constructions like "parts of speech," syntactical forms, and the like, depending on the scientific project we undertake (sociological, psychological, grammatical, whatnot). There is nothing to complain about in all this, if, that is, we are in full awareness of what we are doing, making no claims for conclusions which have bearing on the *concrete* fact of language. Science, said Aristotle, is of the general—which is to say, of the abstract. The concrete is another matter.

In order to speak about speaking (in the concrete), one has to speak. This means that one can never talk about the speech that it takes to speak about speaking. Philosophers who in addition to "seeking the truth" are also truthful in the sense here put forth, will not try to wriggle out of this dilemma, but frankly face it. The infinite regress which here stares one in the face is one that can be resolved only on the model of Aristotle's resolution of the problem of cause or motion. Speaking about speaking about speaking, etc. etc., presupposes a first speech, a *Primum Verbum* which speaks for every speech, and needs not itself to be spoken for—a self-accounting, self-revealing purposing act, in short. Contrary to Aristotle's solution, however, it is not a mere requirement of rational thought which delivers this truth about human speech: the concretely observable fact of art attests to it. We do not have to depend on argument and abstract descriptions of the abstract in this case.

But to go on with what we were saying, how can this full and self-transparent program of purposing which is utterance in its origins be thought of as divorced from practical and from theoretical intentionality? We say that every full utterance contains the quality of a possible whole course of action, as well as a global way of being interested and of feeling. We say that, originally, the possibility *qua* possibility of all this takes form, and that this is exactly what language and aesthetic purposing are about. This poses a double question: How does it happen that an act inwardly designed to serve no purpose other than to make possibility manifest as possibility can be available to be worked on, or to be cast into the mold of other purposing, so that it yields every other form of actuality to our existence besides the aesthetic? What does it mean when this act stays disengaged from other purposing, remaining purely on its own, as in art proper?

As freedom or spontaneity, the act per se of purposing is purposive in two very different senses. It drives for personal identity or "self"-formation, *notwithstanding,* as well as *through,* any and all *roles* it "acts out"; and, it "sets up" the particular roles in and by which it makes these formations actual. Under the latter posture, purposing *has* purposes, or determines itself in choices and decisions; under the former, it is simply itself. "To be a purposing," and to *have* purposes are not the same thing. To be purposing is a condition for having and being at-work-on-purposes, but a being who *is* a purposing does not necessarily have to have purposes, or be working on any particular role-project in order to be itself. "Does not have to," in this context, does not imply that it *may* not, or that it can or cannot do either without doing both It means only that, in order to have purposes, or to determine itself in particular roles, the purposing being must be able to own itself in its own proper being as a purposing, essentially, and that this requires being able to extricate oneself from all roles, or, what amounts to the same thing, being capable of assuming any and all possible roles. In terms of fundamental speech or first utterance, this means that speech cannot but be *personal* before it can be anything else (as personal, in fact, as Van Gogh's sunflowers) but "personal" in the sense in which it is *not yet* yoked to any special practical or theoretical purpose or role. The sense in which Van Gogh's sunflowers may be said to represent a uniquely personal way of speech is not the same as that in which, say, Nikita Khrushchev has expressed his feelings at the United Nations. But the significant difference is not that they were not both "being themselves" by speaking, but that the latter had, obviously, also political commitments to expedite. (To the extent that we can extricate Khrushchev's speech from its political intentions, it would be perfectly proper to consider its purely linguistic or aesthetic import.)

The personal character and uniqueness of the original utterance is such, and presents itself in such a way, that it denotes a purposing which no longer is attending to any special purpose or role. The more precise way of putting this is to say that, in its original utterance, the act of purposing assumes the very peculiar role of self-conscious *"role-player"*—it frees itself from all particular role-playing, so that it can enter into a role which is without practical and theoretical involvement—a free role. Ordinarily, the roles that we assume and enact in thought and in action *possess* us; there is something paranoic or compulsive about every such engagement. And because we *must* appear in such roles to "be what we are," and "not be what we are not," we suffer of necessity, and in our very being, what Jean-Paul Sartre calls *mauvaise foi*—"bad faith." [68] What purposing forgets, and cannot but put aside, is its own very freedom, in order to "be" such roles. (Such roles cannot be assumed at all, except on the pretense that we *are* the role, which cannot really be, since we are the role-player, and not the role played.) The linguistic or aesthetic act permits us to enact our self as free role-player. This it does in and through the actualization of a unique role, but—and here is the mark of its liberating power—as possibility only. The character of sheer possibility of the role here permits what we might call "engagement-without-engagement," or, "engagement-without-pretense." In this case, it is we who possess the role, it does not possess us.

There is a remarkable paradox in all this. It is when the purposing being *becomes* the role, or forces himself whole into it, holding back nothing of himself as free agent that bad faith arises; contrariwise, it is when he is self-possessed as the being who can initiate any and every role that he can "play" the role sincerely and without bad faith. It makes more than just a moral sense to say that Hitler and Mussolini were "bad actors," or that a true actor-artist playing these same roles on the stage would be doing not at all "bad acting," but the genuine article. Also there are those who are inclined to temper their judgment of Mussolini with a note of pity, on grounds that he *was* an actor—a "ham," to be sure—but who look upon Hitler as having been an evil and dangerous man precisely because he was no actor—he really believed himself *to be* the role, and the historical role of the German people as well. Contrary to all appearances, true sincerity and fanaticism are mutually exclusive notions, and not extremes of one and the same thing. The sincere man is not one who merges with his roles, but one rather who plays his role so honestly that he never forgets its status or that it has no other necessity behind it than his own free agency. This is another way of saying that the sincere role

[68] Sartre, *L'Être et le néant*, pp. 85-111.

is one for which we assume absolute personal responsibility because we know we are its enactor.

It may appear that with the introduction of the notions of role and of role-playing, we have diverted from the main subject. The fact of the matter is that this is crucial to the problem of language, art, and personality, existentially considered.[69] For, quite apart from the fact that role-playing can be sincere or insincere, free or fanatical, it is the only way we have of being anything or anybody. There is no purposing without engagement; and even the extreme condition of disengagement called *abulia* is an engagement of a kind. People who pick out one or more among the many roles they have to play in order to live as being peculiarly *their* self can be declaring only where their interests lie (*inter-esse;* what sort of being they *"make matter"*). The fact that some of these honored roles—"father," "friend," "patriot," "scientist," "Christian"—come wrapped in an aura of dignity and approval can indicate only the kind and degree of interest they hold for us: to call them important roles should be sufficient dignification. We must recognize that original utterance is the very act or posture of our being, under which role-playing first arises as very possibility. This is a possibility which is inextricably bound with what we call "personality."

The word "person" originally referred to the actor's mask in the Greek theatre, where characters were identified by a facial mask which also served to magnify sound. The Latin *per-sona* means literally, "that through which there comes sound." This is almost perfect to suggest the exact connection between purposing, role-playing, and speech. The Medieval Latinists added still another significant dimension to the suggestion: they sometimes thought of the Latin word as *per-se-una*—"for one's self." The difficulty in making use of these suggestions is that we might be inclined to intellectualize about them in such a way as to make of the components involved separate entities only mechanically or externally related. We are apt to think of an abstraction called "purposing," of another called "uttering," and then of still another resultant one called "role" or "person," in this or some other order. We would thus be missing the sense of the absolute compresence and contemporaneity of the act.

There is no purposing without utterance of some kind, and no utterance without role or person. Purposing, speaking, and being

[69] *Ibid.*, pp. 115-127.

a person, or being personal, are not to be looked upon as neutral happenings, the "cause" of which lies outside them. Although we can always *find* that we or someone else "has spoken," the concrete fact of the matter is that we *make ourselves speak,* and in the act, also make our "self," or enact the corresponding role. "Speech" that has effectively been made into "everybody's" or "nobody's" "speech" is, of course, a very useful thing for a certain special purpose when we engage in the projects which call for such, but this is not the point where we can catch the living act of speech. By the time speech has been made into everybody's or nobody's, the original living prospectus of possibility which it put forth is already at the service of other engagements, commitments, projects where its fruits are being reaped in other than linguistic ways. However, even here it must not be thought that the original program of possibility first present in the original utterance is no longer active in its own way. It is no merely rhetorical statement to say that Greek science and philosophy represent the carrying out of motifs first fully enacted in Homer, or that one can find the whole of Italian Fascism in the wild utterances of D'Annunzio. Such "working out," or "working on," adds nothing to the original embryo of possibility except translation into practical action, together with the theoretical supports that this calls for. The translation, however, carries inevitably the dangers, as well as the advantages inherent in the necessary depersonification of the originally uttered possibility. By the time the remarkable aesthetic possibility of Greek "Fate" becomes translated into nineteenth century European "Natural Law," we have a new, effective handle over the powers of "nature," but also the ugly face of the loss of personal responsibility, and of nihilism. By the time that the personal utterances of the Hebrew prophets, including Christ, are worked upon, we have not only "salvation," but also utter perdition staring us in the face in the form of impersonal or personally irresponsible claims for the human "Good" backed by the hydrogen bomb.

How strange it is that such momentous occurrences can issue from so innocuous a source as original speech or art. But it is only when we try to see these truths in the large, or in their magnification, that they seem incredible. A closer view of them in smaller matters makes the idea more convincing. A phrase used deprecatingly of women and children is true of all humans: the final honest justification for any of our projects, including the theoretical ones with which we undertake to justify them, is "because," or more exactly, "Because this is the way we sincerely feel." The only thing that saves us from having to make such a frank confession every time is the authority of that same impersonality and anonymity of speech which had its origins in personal honest feeling and imagination. Nevertheless, except for radical, incurable perversion of intention, all humans know the tremendous relaxation of spirit which comes with honest confession. But, one must be able to become a child again, as we say, or a poet—one must be able to find his speech *de novo*—in order to do and say this. One of the undeveloped contentions of this book is that every philosophy, every science, every human undertaking rests finally on some original utterance, some aesthetic realization, coming out of the blue like God's creative *Fiat*.[70] I once asked the philosopher Bowsma how, if he believed in the existence of God, he would go about proving it. He replied (I will never know whether in jest or seriously), "Because God said so!" The same can be said of all that men do or think they are doing: they do it because they say so!

Original utterance is not personal in the sense of being "private" or of concern to him only who utters it. "Speech" that is utterly private is not speech at all, but incipient action parading as speech. There is nothing private about Van Gogh's sunflowers, as everybody knows, and yet, they are certainly personal (so much so, in fact, that we often refer to them simply as "a Van Gogh"). The essence of the personal quality, as well as of all genuine speech is self-disclosure, self-publication, self-announcement. The undeniable fact that the disclosure or announcement is first of all to and of one's self does not make it "private." It has been said over and over again that speech which is not clear or communicative to others must be unformed and unclear to him who is trying to speak. The phenomenon wherein we "feel" we have a great thing to say but "cannot find the words to say it" is quite the same as that in which we feel we have great "symphonies" or "poems" gestating in our souls but know not how to "express" them. The whole of speech and of art lives in the actualization in which it is born: it has nothing to do with projects where ends and means are separated, and so may or may not come together. When we say that something "could have been said more clearly," or in some other way "improved" upon, we are concerned, not with the utterance itself,

[70] The aesthetic origins of science, philosophy, and, perhaps, even religion is a subject so far left untreated by philosophers, though in Croce and Vico certain foundations are laid for such an investigation.

but with the procedures involved in the *recording* of it (we shall
see what such "records" are later on). In this connection, it is well
for us to reflect on the fact that Beethoven can be interpreted very
poorly, passably well, sublimely, or not at all. Nor is this the case
only for arts which, like music or the drama, require rendering
and interpretation. As far as rendering goes, every artist who chooses
to record his creations must be also his own "conductor," "technical director," or "producer." A startling observation (which no
doubt many would naturally be inclined to dispute) is that colored
reproductions of the paintings of certain artists are, in some instances, better than the originals! This seems an absurdity only
when we confuse the ideal work with the "physical" record. Many
truly great artists have been poor technicians, just about good
enough to get by, just as many truly great technicians or artisans
have not been artists at all, though they may have passed as such.

This question of the personal quality of all art and of original
utterance has many dimensions, one worth mentioning again.
This has to do with the muddled idea that there are some things
which "cannot be said," or "talked about." It appears that many
people, on the basis of a narrow and exclusive view of language,
picture for themselves one region of things or states which are, as
they say, "unutterable" and another region of things and states
which somehow can be "communicated." In a famous statement in
his *Tractatus*, the philosopher Wittgenstein says, "About that which
cannot be spoken, one must be silent." As if being silent about
what one knows he cannot speak in any other way were not a pretty
good way of "speaking" about it! Now, apart from the fact that to
say of a thing that it is "unutterable" is actually to say a great deal
about it, there is the patent ambiguity as to whether the "unspeakable" is unspeakable, or something that has nothing at all to do
with speech in the first place, so that no one should associate it with
speech even to the extent of having to say that it is "unspeakable."
Though "labelling" is not exactly speech, it is at least clear that
there can be nothing which cannot be *named* by just inventing a
name for it. If it cannot be said by the spoken word, then, perhaps,
it might be said in painting, in music, or by some gesture. That
everything cannot be spoken in one way—in Oxford English, for
example—does not mean that it cannot be said in the Calabrian
dialect, in the dance, or in sculpture. It is, to be sure, quite useful
to delimit the use of the word "language" for certain specifiable
purposes; but unless one declares these purposes, taking good note

of their limitations, he is apt to engage in irresponsible philosophical massacres in the name of philosophy, on the excuse that one only wants to know what men do with language in particular instances.

It is true that neither art nor speech, even in the original and fundamental sense we are discussing, are everything; and that, whatever there is which is not speech, must be something else. But, we might ask, what can speech be, if not the very thing which is made to lend publicity (in the important, ontological sense) to what is not itself speech? It takes the complete *imbroglio* of supposing that speech can be only either *about* speech, or about what cannot be spoken, to speak about unutterables. Speech about unspeakables has its luminously articulate place in mystical and in poetic utterance, where honest men (contrary to what is sometimes believed) do not engage in mystification, but precisely in the effort of making the as-yet-unuttered utterable. All art and human utterance generally, however recorded, stands witness to the fact that what was once not said is now said. But this does not mean that before it was said the unsaid was there in some form waiting to be declared either sayable or unsayable by philosophers. First utterance is not something which translates the unsaid, or what cannot be said, into speech: it is *its* very word or speech. As for any speculations concerning the absolute whys and wherefores of that which is not speech before it becomes utterance we can well leave it to the metaphysicians and their opponents.

Art as original or first utterance is, then, the first act of *form-giving* to purposing per se, and *form,* properly considered, is the very essence of publicity. In this sense, to be able to utter one's own being, or to be a person, which is the same thing, is to show one's self to oneself, and at the same time or in one and the same act, to-, with-, for-, and if need be, even against-the-world (all that is other-than-one's-self).

The concept of person or personality is, regrettably, too often associated in our minds with exclusiveness, separateness, and insularity. Existentially speaking, we are indeed irremediably alone in our being. But this is not because we are capable of speech or are persons, but precisely because to utter our being, or to give form-giving identity to our being is not gratuitous. It is the capacity to "make speech," and thereby "to make our self," that in a way breaks our loneness of being. Speech opens the door of our dungeon, flooding our self and our world with the first light which permits us to discern both. Before this, we can distinguish no contours, we can perceive no form.

But the original form-giving act is one which gives form to everything at once just as the first vision of the lighted world upon opening the door of a dungeon shows everything at once, without calculated distinctions of real, and unreal, gods or demons. Under the aspect in which this form-giving engenders visible selfhood or personality, it too does so without calculation—as sheer actual-possibility to be breathed, as it were, like the first breath of an infant emerging from the dark womb. And, just as that first breath of the infant establishes all the breaths of his life from that point forth, so also the first utterance and act of form-giving establishes the original pattern—the archetype—of all form-giving. The analogy might help us also to understand how it is that the aesthetic act once born can live its own independent life, however much it may or may not come to be worked on or appropriated for other life-uses.

The fact that the original self-formation of purposing activity is self-and-world-forming in a global way ("shows everything") must not be interpreted to mean that it is vague or general like a concept, which has no individuality. If this were the case, we could hardly associate it with the person. The sense in which it is comprehensive of everything is such that its inclusiveness resides precisely in its absolute uniqueness, its incomparable individuality. In this consists the character of inexhaustibility of the art work. Aesthetic form is thus *monadic* in the Leibnitzian sense, except that it is no metaphysical invention, and is all "window." The first utterance, like the work of art, is a possibility actualized as possibility, carrying within itself all of its compossibles—a complete world of actualized compossibility.[71]

Returning now to the notion of the role, we must distinguish between role-playing (enacting personality or speaking) as it relates to art, and role-playing as it functions in practical life. In what sense

---

[71] Late Medieval Scholastics became involved in a very interesting debate concerning what were called "pure possibles," put forth, it appears, primarily to save human freedom from a view of the divine omnipotence which left little room for it; but, curiously enough, such "pure possibles" were also to save God's omnipotence from human freedom. These possibles, together with their "compossibles," were said to be quite different from purely mental entities (*entis rationes*) which had their existence in the mind; they were supposed to have their being in God's intellect, and had no need to ever exist in any other way. See P. Benedetto D'Amore, O.P., "La metafisica del nulla e dell'essere di M. Heidegger" in *Sapienza*, Roma, Anno 9, No. 4-5, pp. 368-369.

are Van Gogh's sunflowers personal, and disclosing of unique personality? In what sense is his amputation of his ear something personal and revealing of the person of Van Gogh? It would be too simple to say that both these doings represent, in the same way, different things that Van Gogh did in order to be himself. It would be an over-simplification also to say that in both these doings we find and have an intimate encounter with the same person. Unless Van Gogh was playing a part in some drama when he cut off his ear (which is unlikely), the personality disclosed by this act (or any report of such) is not one in which we can recognize our own selves by re-enacting it. There is something unshareable, really private (because it is action and not speech) about such enactment of purposing; we remain forever outsiders to it. (But, of course, Van Gogh's self-mutilation has become legend—that is, has itself taken on aesthetic character—and in this sense only can we share it or empathize with it.) Quite a different thing is the "doing" we call Van Gogh's "sunflowers." This comes disattached from the historical Van Gogh's "personal" involvements and interests, and in fact is personality which, like a part or role in a play, available to anyone who wants to play it, can be entered into as if into one's own self. This is not to say that Van Gogh had two personalities—one which cut off his ear, the other the painter of sunflowers. Rather, he, like all men, both made his roles for their own sake—as sheer possibilities of being—and played out other roles in actual life. Role-playing, in other words, can—indeed, must—be enacted on its own account, "disinterestedly," before we can act out any roles in the sense of existential involvements in action. Role-playing must be free or spontaneous before it can be existentially engaged in and, also, that such free or spontaneous role-playing can be enacted for its own sake, and without concern for the carrying out of practical programs of action. Under the second of these purposing postures, each man is entrusted with the making of the very models of selfhood for himself and for all others, without which there can be no selfhood at all, aesthetic or otherwise.[72] And this is a posture which intrinsically involves sharing.

Van Gogh's sunflowers offer a public, available opportunity to be-a-self-in-its-world, without strings attached, and with no com-

[72] This is made central to an existential ethics in a work in preparation by the author: *The Quest for Concreteness*. See, P. A. Schilpp, "On the Nature of the Ethical Problem," *The International Journal of Ethics*, Vol. XLVII, No. 1, Oct. 1936.

pulsion to mobilize will or reason in order to put the role into practice. From the point of view of original language, it represents something that anybody and everybody can say *for himself*, a *persona* through which he can make his own personal sound without having to merge with the program of purposing which is presented as pure possibility. As such, original utterance or art is truly what Nietzsche suggested—a power which not only makes it possible for "man to be reconciled with his fellow, but actually to become one with him." For it makes possible a unity—a reciprocity and mutuality of personal identification—which otherwise could never be. It is by virtue of this fundamental fluidity of being-and-knowing-selfhood in its infinite variety that we are able not only to taste (the French and Italian words for "to know" are *savior* and *sapere* —from the Latin *saporem*, "to taste") the infinite possibilities of our own personal being, as well as the ontological bond which unites us to all purposing being. It is by this power and capacity that we can know what it is like to be Hamlet-in-his-world, or Don Quixote in his. And what is even more important, it is by this power and capacity that we can have identity of personal being with both "God" and "Satan," with the good man and the thief, the madman and the sane man, all of which are inseparable in the concrete situations of our existence. In this way, art prepares us to act properly the real role of judges, since the judge who does not know what it is like to be the thief cannot judge the thief.[73] And it is precisely because, aesthetically speaking, the role of the thief can be entered into, and inwardly lived out as an actual possibility—freely—that it can effectively constitute and deepen our essential humanity. Intellectual and practical appraisals and descriptions of thievery in themselves prepare no one to be human, let alone to be a judge.

It should be clear that role-enactment, insofar as it enjoys the freedom or spontaneity of the aesthetic posture in purposing, has immeasurably wider scope and reach than in its historical executions. There is here a natural excess, an overflowing as in a fountain which pours its fresh waters even when the villagers are asleep or have no use for water. And, if we may extend the figure, it is because no one thinks of putting a faucet on the fountain that the water is ever fresh. Unfortunately, the tendency to consider the excess a waste is strong in humans, and so, the font of spontaneous being is forever being shut off in the practical course of

[73] See pp. 132-136.

living. Attending to, and prizing the aesthetic in our existence is like valuing the superabundance which keeps the source clean.

It would seem, at first view, that some men do art, and some do not—that art is a specialization which engages only some men. When this distinction is not merely superficial, it is only useful for certain purposes, like those which engage art collectors, museum directors, and art dealers. The fact is that what appears to be a specialization in aesthetic purposing is one, actually, in the making of certain records, which have not always to do with art.[74] The artist considered as "one who paints pictures," "composes music," or "writes poetry," is a man who in addition to doing what everybody else does when he functions aesthetically also engages in certain actions or composite of actions whose traces or tracings, so to speak, other men find of use—not necessarily just for what we have called the aesthetic enactment, but for all sorts of other reasons as well. Such tracings can serve as financial investments, like stocks and bonds; for "showing off" one's riches; or even for pretense or poseur as artist or art connoisseur. It is possible that fully ninety-nine per cent of the millions of "pieces" made under the name of art each year in the art schools, clubs, and other art associations in this country, have little use or value only to inflate egos, console bored people, or relieve sexual anxieties.

The schematized actions and their tracings which go to make up the physical thing we call "work of art" have, of course, their own kind of justification and importance, which we do not mean to minimize in any way. Such a feat, like any other useful operation, involves much preparation, "aptitude," and often much sacrifice for the person who undertakes it. It involves knowledge and "knowhow" which is not easy to come by, even where the evidences of such effort are obscured by the simplicity of the construction. (People who say of certain modern art that "a child could have done it!" hardly realize that they are really complimenting both the artist for the spontaneity of his execution, and the child for his aesthetic power!) As maker, simply, of the physical gadget—the art-*thing,* the sincere artist should, of course, be praised, which is what we all do every time we admire what we call the "technique" of certain artists. The trouble is that while Mantegna and David, for examples, have techniques which arouse our admiration and give us much to talk about, Matisse and Picasso (at least in some of their periods) have not. When we try to make an extended and

[74] See Chapter Five.

important issue out of "technique," we quickly verge on other, non-technical characteristics, such as the "violence of the color," the "delicacy of the brush-stroke," and other such things which have directly to do with the concrete elements and relations in the work of art proper. What might be called the "classical abstractionist technicalists" in aesthetic criticism seem always at a complete loss when confronted with certain modern poetry and art—Eliot's *Waste Land,* or the paintings of Pollock, for examples. True, something can always be said about the technique of any artist, but this can never go very far in regard to any significant explication of the aesthetic work as such.

If there is anything which makes the appellation "artist" more appropriate for certain men than for others, it is not that they can do what the others cannot do, but that they somehow care to have commerce about what they do with other men. The existing tracings or records of aesthetic vision at any time are certainly never any sure indication that even greater or more significant aesthetic creations have not occurred without ever being recorded. We may well regret it when men either have not or choose not to use the ability to record their creations for mankind, as we must honor those who are both willing and capable of doing this. The willingness or the capacity to make such a record, however, is not in itself an aesthetic matter, but as we believe, at bottom, a moral and utilitarian one. The moral responsibility involved can best be understood when we consider the ever-present possibility of the insincere creeping into, and disguising itself as art, and when we understand that art is no pastime, but very serious existential business.

Still we can make use of the distinction between artist and non-artist in a way which leads us directly into another aspect of the subject under discussion. All men are not similarly alive and active in the spontaneity of their being. With some, spontaneity surges rebelliously and is pivotal to their lives, while with others, it is so subdued and lethargic that they can hardly be said to be alive to the fact of being alive. Between these extremes, the great majority of men occupy, as we may well suppose, some middle position on a scale of degrees of fundamental spontaneity. The artist is one who not only occupies the higher ranges of the scale, but also finds the greatest need to expend his freedom or spontaneity with sublime prodigality. But above all he is also one who profoundly needs *free* association with others; *i.e.,* he needs love more than other men.

The artist more than other men needs to find his being in all possible roles, and needs also to assure himself that others share this free making of self-identity with him. In this respect, he is the eternal paragon and very model of *humanism,* Wagner and Gaugin notwithstanding. (The essence of humanism is not self-effacement, but the glorification of selfhood as opposed to ego.[75])

ART AS THE RENEWAL OF SPONTANEITY

The artist more than other men has a strong sense of what we have called the *nostos* and the *pathos* of existence. He feels and is impelled more strongly than others by the sense of radical incompleteness of his existence and by the submerged memory of what it is like *really to be* (of making actuality per se). Aesthetic sensitivity can be subsumed under these headings, for it has basically to do with a profound dissatisfaction with all theoretical and practical resolutions of the problem of existential being, and with a submerged memory of what it is like to be the absolute freedom which stands behind being itself—to be that which alone could account for its very possibility. The artist is the ontological *magus* of the spontaneous.

It is our purpose now to speak of art as the fundamental act wherein purposing itself endures, persists, or remains self-identical in renewing itself *qua* spontaneity. Spontaneity is not another project of purposing activity like the others, but the act itself of purposing, for whatever end.

To indicate once again the difference between spontaneous and unspontaneous activity I shall recall something said to me about the physicist Enrico Fermi by a mutual friend. During the days when the first atomic fission was being worked on in the converted Stag Stadium of the University of Chicago, a remarkable group of scientific men were gathered to work on the project in great secrecy. The work sessions were held in a dusty room, where each morning the scientists gathered to fill the blackboards with mathematical equations. Most often the sessions began with great enthusiasm, as if all felt that they were on the verge of making the great discovery, and ended in the evening with cluttered blackboards and some discouraging impasse. Fermi (who eventually was responsible for the

75 Wagner and Gaugin were notoriously self-centered.

first successful fission) was the most taciturn, making only hesitant and rare comments during the sessions. Usually, when the meetings had reached the point of fatigue, Fermi would say something in his soft voice which startled everyone by its seeming total ir-relevancy and almost childish simplicity. The person who re-ported this story said: "It was as if someone had turned on the light in a dark room, showing new and unsuspected possibilities for a whole new world of ideas."

Whatever it was about Fermi's intromissions that renewed the collective scientific effort and opened new vistas, it would be dif-ficult to account for it all in terms merely of what is called "sci-entific knowledge." For it was precisely such knowledge that be-came, as it were, freed from its own dead weight, expanded in new directions by Fermi's remarks. It would be better to say that new science actually came into being because of the remarks. In the same way, aesthetic purposing renews human existence and all of its efforts, providing fresh vision, novel intentionality, and (often disconcerting to entrenched interests) deflation of the presumed importance of our engaged-projects.

The fact that Daumier's court scenes, or Goya's prints about the horrors of war are not direct incentives to action (great art never is) must not mislead us into thinking that they have not latent in them the power to remodel human purposing with respect to how humans feel about injustice, or about the obscenity which is war. (Who can tell how many times humans have actually been trans-formed in their very souls by encounter with these aesthetic visions?) Nor must we be deceived by the fact that a great deal of art seems to have little or no connection with any recognizable projects such as justice or war. Our outlook and general attitude on life itself is also a project—perhaps the most fundamental of all our projects in which all the others find their life-breath. And there is not a single work of art, not a single first utterance, which does not, in its own way, present us with at least a possibility of novel outlook and global perspective. What counts here is that this—if it is truly aesthetic, and if we truly are able to enact it—is a concrete and actual possibility, one that is *tasted,* fused with one's very being in the enactment. No man who really encounters Cézanne's apples ever sees apples again in the same way, just as no man who really reads Sartre's *The Wall* or Camus' *The Stranger* can look upon death and our contemporary values as he did before the encounters. It is true that a great majority of gallery- and theatergoers, no less than readers of novels, seem to be little transformed by their experiences—but if they have any kind of aesthetic sensitivity, who can measure the degree of transformation they truly have undergone by such experiences? One would have to follow them throughout their lives, watch their every decision, hear their every utterance in order to be able to judge.

But, of course, there is with us also the dull and insensitive human who has either only very superficial aesthetic experiences or none at all. The kind of man who particularly must interest us, however, is the complete victim of conformism, the Institutionalized Man in whom the Institution has succeeded in pouring the immobilizing lead of the "true," the "good," and the "beautiful" according to prescription. The principal characteristic of this kind of man is a certain remarkable dexterity in keeping separate the things that are interdependent and inseparable. This is the man who buys seasonal tickets to the concert, but does not appreciate the beauty of his wife's speaking-voice; who reads Henry Miller with avidity but makes love to his wife by schedule in darkness, and in the assured crumb of salvation which comes from properly condemning himself for doing it, or for any excess passion. He is the man who can carry on a fairly intelligent conversation on the *Sermon on the Mount,* but day-dreams of disembowelling Mr. Khrushchev or the Rev. Martin Luther King personally; and who reads *The Grapes of Wrath* with relish, but who simply *knows* that "the minimum wage law is just another step toward communism." Such a man has his values sharp and clear. The aesthetic runs off him like water off a duck's back. For such a man, art is completely irrelevant to the business of living ("business is business"). A closer look would certainly reveal this kind of man to be the most representative product of that mercantile mentality of which Erich Fromm speaks.[76] Except for a few irrepressible rebels in prison, and some art creators who are fortunate enough to be considered only puzzling or amusing, this man is ubiquitous and everywhere, a dictator of other's values. Something of this kind of man is in all of us who are, and must be, "respectable."

Because of the separation and lack of unification of roles, the unspontaneous man is not one, but many; he is a noisy crowd rather than a single personality. Hence, too, he is in perennial conflict—a conflict which forces upon him the most stringent self-

[76] Erich Fromm, "Love in America" in Huston Smith, ed., *The Search for America* (Englewood Cliffs, N.J.: Prentice-Hall, Inc., 1959), pp. 123-131.

surveyance, if he would hold the pieces together. He must talk fast and continuously, in that inner dialogue with oneself that we call thought, so that he can silence whatever original utterance may still burgeon in him. If he hangs together at all in his conflicting parts, it is due to no self-renovating inward spontaneity of purpose, but precisely to a studied and systematized practice of escaping renewal. This stultifying feat he is usually best able to accomplish in association with other men, where the others' noises are added to his own to produce a din which makes his waning ability to speak sincerely to himself altogether ineffectual. This divided and self-oblivious state fuses him with what Heidegger calls *Das Mann,* the epitome of depersonification, where he reaps all the benefits of individual irresponsibility, others' approval, and of course, material security. He is then the "one-hundred-percenter" of what-ever you like. Nor must it be thought that this thing-state he achieves is one lacking in any of the ingredients which go to make up the authentic person: the ingredients are all there, only they are fraudulent. Thus, the unauthentic man has the conscience suited to his role: the conscience of unfreedom, whose distinguishing mark is incapacity for self-forgiveness (and, therefore, incapacity to forgive others). In the same way, the unauthentic man has "strength of character," "fundamental commitments," and all the other trappings which we associate with the fully developed person; his "character," however, reflects the cruelty of self-righteous mediocrity, and his "commitments" are forever the issue of ungenerous cal-culation.[77]

We can here make use of the Latin root in the word "spon-taneous." namely *sponte*—"of one's own accord"—to say that un-spontaneous activity is "not of one's own accord," or peculiarly self-disowning, and hence, ungenerous in its very nature. It resists its own impulses, blocks itself in any effort to *give itself out,* remaining prisoner in its own act, by its own hand, as it were. But this sense of "generous" has little to do with philanthropy, tolerance, or any-thing else which represents acting with intent to accomplish some-thing. This is generosity in purposing itself, or doing something for no purpose whatsoever, even including "being generous." Any illustration we might give of this ontological generosity—this *being-generously*—must seem strange, for it is not of the sort that might be suggested by speaking of giving up something which one prizes, or allowing something to be, in which one does not himself find

[77] See also A. B. Fallico, *The Quest for Authentic Existence,* pp. 73-77.

his being or even understanding," and "being able to imagine" what something possibly can be like. This is, rather, being able to put one's self forth as the very possibility embodied in feeling and imagination.[78] This is the sense in which one has to be generous in order to reveal himself to himself, and to reveal also other selves as one's own self. It contains the element of unselectivity, of un-prejudice. What comes to be so intimately owned or accepted is not here first measured for size, or made to fit one's preferences; one, rather, expands or contracts his very being, naturally and without effort, in order to fit into it, finding his preference in the act. Spontaneous being is generous in the way that the Brahman of the Upanishads is said to be generous in his "playful" periods, when he evolves into new worlds. It is utterly irrelevant to ask why he does it. Spontaneity is moved neither by gain nor by loss. All pre-conceptions and anticipations, in fact, impair its course, or stop it in its tracks altogether.

Seeking to discover the secret of her strange poetry, I once asked Gertrude Stein why she wrote as she did. Her reply was, "Because I get pregnant and have to deliver myself of the child!" Such an answer seemed, at the time, as strange as Gertrude Stein's poetry, but whatever may be the value of the poetry, and whatever she may have meant by her answer, something important can be made of it in this connection. Spontaneity bears resemblance to par-turition at least in this respect: one cannot fake it, and it brings new life into being out of one's self. Moreover, one is wholly preg-nant or not pregnant at all.

Spontaneity unifies, clears purposive activity of its own obstruc-tions, and returns it to its own primal springs.[79] Taken altogether, we refer to these reformations of the act as renewal of spon-taneity. The expression "re-birth" would, no doubt, better serve in this connection, on account of its ambivalence of meaning: to be born implies "coming into being ever anew." What we have is the full sense of that existential *repetition* which occupied us earlier. By this *repetition,* purposing maintains itself in its Role of Roles, which is freedom itself, by positing its free act ever anew— new, paradoxically, because ever the same, and the same, because ever new and different.

[78] Our view bears resemblance to Aristotle's doctrine of Catharsis in the *Poetics,* but it relates to existential being itself, rather than the emotions.
[79] B. Croce, *La filosofia di Giambattista Vico* (Bari: Laterza e Figli, 1933), pp. 127, 137.

It was Giambattista Vico who first took serious note of the renovating character of aesthetic purposing. Applying this idea to
historical process as a whole, Vico saw history moving in a spiral
course, each phase starting afresh in a return (*ricorso*) to what he
called "barbarism," by which he meant a pre-moral, pre-reflective,
or poetic beginning. Thus, for Vico, the poetic mind stands ever
at the beginning, like the fountain of youth wherein history and
culture find their eternal rejuvenation after every formation, which
naturally culminates in wearysome and sterile old age, or intellectual and scientific over-sophistication. His *ricorso* is something
of a new lease on life. What is interesting in all this is that Vico
saw the practical and intellectual developments in the human
situation as naturally and unavoidably leading to old age, ex-
haustion, and death. The creative energies, he saw as renewable
only in the first or original utterance of poetry.

How does purposive activity come to lose its spontaneity? By
what regression does it become a wasteland of unproductivity, a
land for strangers? It would be in the spirit of Vico to say, simply,
that there can never be, in any practical and theoretical program
or formation of human purpose, any more than was contained in
the first aesthetic utterance and vision which gave it birth. When
the possibilities are worked out, when the aesthetic word has received all its translations and commentaries, the spring runs dry.
There is no way of quickening the dying hulk into new life, except
as the blood of spontaneity can again run through its veins. But
bodies dying of degenerative old-age diseases are not easily healed
by transfusions, even of young blood. New, original possibilities
are needed to replace the old and spent ones. And here a twofold
difficulty always arises: the new and replenishing possibilities are
hard to discern with old eyes and hard to embrace with tired
atrophied arms; and they must be available to begin with.

Under these circumstances, the old and the new overlap—often
living together without vital contact. The aesthetic man is the
stranger, the outsider, amidst a world in which the suicidal and the
absurd become progressively more desperately active in proportion
as they become more self-contradictory and impossible. It is then
that *Guernica* appears like something from another world, even as
the Spanish Civil War unfolds into the Hitler madness, while the
"good men and true" go on "talking of Michelangelo" [80] as if
nothing was happening. Under this form, the work of aesthetic

[80] T. S. Eliot, "The Love Song of J. Alfred Prufrock."

purposing is at once both prophetic and rebellious. Often, too, it
is a burst of sardonic laughter—a "dadaism." The aesthetic surge
and hunger for new vision may then become a veritable convulsion,
an epileptic fit. The artist may even pick up the stuff itself which
is decaying and exhibit it untouched before a world which expresses
its secret nausea of it by evincing amusement at the sight. The artist
will compress old automobile junk and place the squeezed mess on
a pedestal, even as he will tell without comment the absurd story
of Roquentin or Meursault. In their desperation as whole men,
even artists will seek cover from the stench they have helped to expose perhaps in some Eliotian conversion, thereby confessing
depletion even of the aesthetic font. But neither art nor life are
ever renewed by escaping from freedom.[81]

This whole phenomenon remains the same when we look at it
in the small. When the world collapses around the existing man;
when every project, every philosophy becomes unconvincing and
uneliciting of one's deepest and sincerest commitment; when a man's
subjective and personal being becomes only externally attached
to his own life-world like an air mail stamp on a meaningless letter
returned to him, his spontaneous moments are all the justification
that remains for his still "being around." Such moments, too, are
both prophetic and potentially revolutionary. What remains of one's
capacity to be truthful gnaws at one's very being in the face of all
the objective "truths" on which the petrified institution of life
rests. But the subjective truthfulness persists in all the sham *mise
en scène*, the central role of a man makes its presence felt amidst
all the masks through which he must still "make sounds," if he
would "get along," "not be bothered," be "thought well of," or
even stay meaninglessly alive. The man revisits his own private
fount of spontaneity in secret, often in disguise even from himself
in moments when he can be and do "of his own accord." In the
midst of all the meaningless talk which he must pour out, he also
speaks out of the generosity of his very being, even if only on rare
occasions, and is himself surprised by what he hears himself say.
Often, too, in the desperate need to be himself against all the pretense and the lying, he utters to himself the honest though frenzied
and mad word, rejecting existence itself as unbearable hell. For,
there are times when the nihilism of suicide, contemplated as
aesthetic possibility, seems to be the only meaning that life can

[81] Karl Shapiro, "T. S. Eliot: The Death of Literary Judgment," *Saturday
Review*, Vol. XLIII, (Feb. 27, 1960).

have (the execution of such a possibility is, of course, nothing aesthetic, but an engaged life-project, even as contemplation of suicide as part of the act of committing it is also something non-aesthetic).

Renewal of spontaneity is nothing that can be instituted "by deliberation"; it is not another choice as with ordinary projects. As was pointed out earlier, freedom in the sense of spontaneity is not the same as "freedom of choice." [82] In order for one to choose freely, or to exercise what is called freedom of choice, one must first be free in the sense of being a spontaneous being. For the man who is unfree, a prisoner of himself, can also make what are called free choices; that is, he can engage himself with one rather than another project. But he can do this always in and through the same unrenovated role, or with an unfreed self. Those who say that a criminal like Hitler was morally responsible because he had free choice and knew what he was doing say this usually on the basis of an ethics and a conception of human freedom which, in addition to making Hitler responsible for his choice of projects, cannot also make him responsible for *the kind of man he made himself into,* which is the thing that was really determinative of his choice of projects.[83] Most all traditional ethics is vitiated by this very misconception. This also is what usually makes of ethics itself just another ulteriorly motivated project whose fundamental purpose remains unspoken and hidden—merely an extension of political, economic, or other interests already espoused. In this we have the formula for the self-impairment of freedom or spontaneity: when we attempt to resolve the conflict of purposes which inevitably grow out of the execution of any theoretical-practical program of living, by forcing any one of the very roles which are causing the trouble, we get deeper and deeper into trouble, deepening also the chasm which has developed between what we need to be, and what we think we are or must be.

Our misconceptions with regard to freedom in the true sense derive principally from two sources: our unwillingness to pull out of projects in which we feel we already have found the actualization of the self which gives us sense of being, and the dread of assuming the Role of Roles—that of being makers of our self or being the freedom that we are. Hence it is that the re-enactment of spontaneity which the aesthetic represents involves not so much an "act of will" as it does "putting the will aside"; i.e., extricating ourselves

[82] *Vide ante,* pp. 5-6.
[83] Croce, *Filosofia della pratica* (Bari: Guis. Laterza e Figli, 1932), p. 36.

from interested action and theory ("interested," let us recall, means "to find being therein," or "to make it so it matters"). Spontaneity is thus regained or re-enacted by relaxing our hold on life, or giving ourselves that new "grace" or "chance" of which Vico spoke in connection with his *ricorso*. It takes an act of self-kindness and self-understanding—an Executive Pardon—to free ourselves from our own self-made prisons and sentence of spiritual death. This fact certain contemporary motivation or depth psychiatry already understands very well, even if most philosophy, like the contemporary technologist and the politician continues to hunt for objective engines or contraptions, intellectual or physical, that will usher in the new world. The living art of any epoch, whether in the sense of the specially recorded formations of artists, or in the wider sense of the aesthetic creativity of existing men generally, shows how this trans-humanization can be. It does so, sometimes rebelliously, by showing up or exposing in its pure possibility of being the bleak world of the unfree and unspontaneous; at other times, by some positive utterance which stands as a new world of possibilities ready to be enacted in what we call real life. But, in any case, it stands present always as reminder of our own capacity and power to *utter* reality, rather than merely to describe it, or to act on it.

It is no mere historical coincidence that every revolutionary transformation of human societies, every concerted undertaking, every culture, can be found as the coiled-up embryo of an aesthetic possibility antecedently actualized in works of art. Homer contains all the archetypes of what we know as Greek civilization—its science, its philosophy, its politics, and all its values. The lamentations of the Hebrews, including the sublimely childlike and hopeful utterance of the Jew, Christ, contains all that part of Christian civilization which is not from Greek, or Roman. Always the new and different life is delivered by a new and different *kind of man* who first envisions himself, or takes form in the disclosures of art. It is also true that each new kind of man and new culture builds its final epitaph in a closing aesthetic effort, and that these very epitaphs are then often re-enacted, re-shaped, filled with new vigor, and turned once again into novel sources of living and of valuing.

What usually is not easily or clearly distinguishable from within the immediate contexts of history is what is the live source and what the gravestone, so that there invariably arises with the un-

spontaneous man, a Cult of the Dead, which seeks to entomb the
very source of all spontaneity. It is then that the "is's" and the "is
not's," the "ought's" and the "ought not's" issuing from their lairs
in the theories and the practices of men become extended to the
very origination of feeling and imagination without which actuality
itself becomes cadaverous and altogether silent about the freedom
that is man. Moreover, the pernicious thing about such necromancy
is not that its followers are not able to enact the funereal celebration which is the "classical" art to which they are dedicated,
but that they misuse the enactment or use it only to keep themselves and others from re-enacting spontaneity afresh. But every
epoch has its "progressive" and its "conservative" tempers; and this
applies not only to how men feel about the records of aesthetic
purposing, but also to how they feel about everything else. Thus,
a rebellious *avant garde* is never lacking, even if it goes unnoticed,
is persecuted, or is ridiculed out of the main current of life and
into the squalid attics of our rotting cities.

A closer look at the main phenomenon we are now observing
shows some revealing genealogies, often not even suspected. In
Euripides, there is present that self-awareness of the subjective
individual which is found fullblown and embodied in the Stoic,
Christian, and later conceptions of man. The Medieval cathedral,
no less than the closely measured and realistically imaged *Divine
Comedy* herald that empirical and mathematical outlook on reality
which finds its life-translation in the post-Medieval world. It is no
mere coincidence that physiology and anatomy first took analytic
form in the work of the Italian Renaissance artist, and that so
much of modern physics and astronomy stems from that same concern for optics which, on the aesthetic side, first engaged the
painters of the Rennaissance. The psychoanalytic movement and
all that it involves is first seen in the subtle presentations of the
French *précieux* literature, and the whole of the evolutionist movement has its aesthetic counterpart in Romantic literature. Italian
Futuristic art projected the possibility of sleek modern design
wedded to speed, and the French Cubists anticipated the geometrical
perspectives of space travel.

But because art is always mirror as well as molder, Dante re-
capitulates the Medieval world, and Shakespeare exhibits its final
outcome in existential doubt, ghosts, and disillusionment; Hemingway, together with countless others among the "exiles," exposes the
castration and impotency of the modern world, and Kafka together

with Camus show the absurd face of that world; the surrealists reveal with paranoic clarity the irrationality and amorality of that same world, and the American non-objective expressionists put on exhibit its utter depersonification and dehumanization.

Such prospective-retrospective reference of art, if at all noticed by the art critics and the aestheticians, is taken much too lightly. And this is because both art criticism and aesthetics generally have disregarded the fact that all our tangible reality has its being and its end in the gained syntheses of feeling and image, which are delivered by aesthetic purposing in its renewals of spontaneity. To the grave and serious mind it must always seem that so un-reflective a thing as art cannot possibly play so fundamental and constitutive a role in human affairs. Nevertheless, "A journey of a thousand miles," said Lao-tse, "is started with a single step."

In what sense can we say that the retrospective, the mirror-role of art is also renovating of spontaneity, or (which is the more appropriate way of asking the question), what part does the mirroring play in the renewal of spontaneity? This question refers us back to the existential problem of repetition as this enters into the maintenance of continuity in the self-identification of existential being. Concrete repetition, we said, is one in which novelty and sameness arise together. Now, the endurance of the self-same involves not only a "memory" of what has been or of the previous formation, but an actualization of it in the *now* in which it becomes fused with the novel projection of possibility (the concrete now *is* this fusion or synthesis). In order to be preserved, as it must, such memory must be identified, made present as a whole or grasped as something completed. "The owls of Minerva fly at eventide" for art as for philosophy, as Hegel said. Art is the insight that only mature age can have of its own youth. Thus, just as molder or giver of form, aesthetic purposing is prospective and daring, as mirror and recapitulator of purposing that is spent, it is composedly contemplative and evaluative in its own way. But both sides of the dialectic deliver only possibility as such: what is past is shown in what was really in it as pure possibility or as a free essence. This point is important, because there are many ways of bringing the past to bear on present concerns which have nothing to do with the aesthetic as such. It is important because much "aesthetic" concern with the past upon inspection turns out to be the work of tendentious purposing posing as art. The undistinguished statues of athletes surrounding Mussolini's Forum in Rome speak more for the fakery of his Fascism than they do for the spirit of ancient Rome. An enormous amount of representational painting and portrature may serve as accurate or inaccurate history, but it is not art. Authentically aesthetic repossessions of the historical life are on the order of Picasso's *Guernica,* Hemingway's *For Whom the Bell Tolls,* or Beethoven's *Eroica.* In sum, the re-actualization of the past in art renews spontaneity because it is a free repossession of it in the essential pure possibility out of which it originally sprang—a possibility which is memorative of the condition of the being who was capable of making his selfhood therein. Repossession of the past in this sense entirely resolves the old self into the new and emerging one: it spells out the "re" in "renewal," and is an integral part of the very structure of self-transcendence. There is here no regression, no retreat into the old, but a revitalization of the past yielding liberation from the past itself. An analogy for this is in the psychoanalytical procedure, where the patient is said to accept and to take over his own past, no matter what it has been, and to re-establish his freedom, or to free himself from compulsions thereby. The analogy serves to show also that the inner intent of aesthetic purposing is not to institute the past as archetype and form-giver for future purposing, but as confirmation that the live creator of form in its very possibility is still present and active, however confused or disowning of himself he may be. It is in this way that art offers us an "interpretation" of the past which is the most honest, just because the most free and disinterested.

All this can be summed up in the simplest terms by saying that the renewal of the very springs of feeling and imagination involves a moment of repossession of the act itself which has made its presence in the already felt and the already imagined.

ART AND REBELLION

The renewal of spontaneity is as painful and agonizing as it is relieving or cathartic. For whether in the existing man or in society, where the impulse and the need "to be one's self" is stirring, the contrary impulse to stay entrenched in purposing already self-formed and explicating itself into practical life is present also. The ensuing battle must forever be an unequal one. The reactionary forces fight from familiar and established ground, where ready-made theories and practices arm and shield men against the terrible responsibility of being or enacting the freedom that they are, and where creature satisfactions and the self-fulfillment of the overflowing trough hold the best prospects for giving meaning to existence. Under these circumstances, the renewal of spontaneity in purposing entails the pains of self-delivery, with the added complication that the unborn child is unwanted, or even opposed as an enemy.

In itself, aesthetic purposing is neither rebellious nor conforming insofar as the engaged projects of life are concerned. Aesthetic purposing never pretends to settle the issues of practice or theory in living. It can, of course, be present with or accompanied by extra-aesthetic purposings and projections, but it remains aesthetic not because, but in spite of this. Thus much of Rivera's murals are open propaganda for and against political and economic interests, but it is not in this that Rivera's art resides. One might as well argue that the Sistine Chapel murals of Michelangelo have their aesthetic worth as posters for the Roman Catholic dogmas. Again, much of Edgar Guest's "poetry" is nothing more than sentimental propaganda for certain middle-class values, but there is no art in it. Aesthetic purposing can come associated with good, bad, or indifferent causes; but if it is at all present, it can always be extricated as something on its own account. If it can be said to be rebellious or revolutionary as art, we must locate this character elsewhere, and in a different way.

It is best that our illustrations be conspicious, for here, too, obviousness conceals what is in plain view. What is the sense in which it can be said that Camus' *The Stranger*, for example, protests against something, or speaks for rebellion? Suppose we say that Camus, through or by use of the story of Meursault, is saying something like this: "Contemporary European man has lost his bearings, his values, and his very humanity. Life is something that happens to him; he no longer makes anything happen, and what is even more significant, he no longer cares. He is surrounded by a world of absurdities, of insincerity, of impersonal forces which taken all together represent the Hangman, leading only to the scaffold. European man no longer determines anything, and is lost in a sea of absurdities, trivia, and fraudulent values. Let him return to the simple, direct sensualism which will at least fill his moment with honest pleasure; let him proclaim with Nietzsche, 'Let me be true to the earth!' rejecting all the pious lies of existence."

The trouble with this assertion is that nowhere in *The Stranger* does Camus say anything like this or, what is even more important, slyly suggest it. A set of statistics, together with some pertinent sociological and psychological descriptions would have accomplished his purpose much more effectively had he so intended.

Phenomenologically considered, *The Stranger* is neither a description, nor an argument *about* anything. Its being is self-contained and fully displayed just as it is: we are referred to nothing beyond it. If we are inclined to use it to go beyond, or to consider something else *through* it, as we would use a pair of colored spectacles, this is nobody else's business but our own.

The Stranger is an organism of felt-images which constitute the whole and actual presence of a possibility of being-a-self-in-its-life-world. That this being-a-self-in-its-life-world (being-Meursault-in-his-life-world) is associated with twentieth century Europe, with a certain individual living in a certain place at a certain time under such and such circumstances, in no way makes the story into a factual report of historical events. The temporal and spatial restrictions of the art presentation belong to the presentation itself. To the presentation itself belong also any "judgments" made on man and his life in the twentieth century—they are internal to the organism of felt images.

Now, as felt-imaged possibility of a self-in-its-life-world, *The Stranger* can have its being only in the enactment by an existing individual. It does not exist in the abstract (though, of course, abstractions called "The Stranger" can always be intellectually set up, as we are doing at this very moment for the purposes of the present philosophical or non-aesthetic side of our project). Moreover, the enactment we are referring to is quite a different thing from what is ordinarily meant by "identification-with." Identification with the character Meursault, for example, as when while reading the novel we imagine ourselves to be Meursault because we like him or because we would wish to have happen to us what happens to him, is not the identification or enactment which here concerns us. Such identification is not essentially aesthetic, but wish-fulfilling. In the aesthetic enactment, we "become" the role out of no ulterior or secret motives whatsoever: It resolves none of our problems, vicariously or otherwise. The aesthetic enactment is on the order rather of an *ontological collaboration,* a disinterested venturing into the making of possible selfhood-in-its-life-world for its own sake. We do not here have to hold back ourselves, our spontaneity, keeping watch over the role and the role-playing to make sure that we do not really believe, as wish-fulfilling and vicarious living always require. Awareness of and attention to the "real" and the "unreal" evaporate, because they play no part in the aesthetic enactment. If we speak of "identification," we must say that this is identification with the whole-in-all-its-parts, and not with some selected character, or certain of the events presented. The identification is with the *activity of making* self-in-its-life-world, rather than with the fact (the "made" considered as such). This is a crucially important point.

The element of revolt in *The Stranger* must be sought—not in anything that can be extracted from the enactment by way of theories, judgments, facts, and the like—but in the concrete activity itself which it is. And this activity is the whole of it. The element of revolt does not even reside in some particular emotion which is inciting to extra-aesthetic actions, or to some comparison that can be made between what is presented in the work, and the condition of the real world. It resides only in the recovery which it permits of the act of spontaneity itself—the original form-giving act. But it is always in that particular and unique way of the particular enactment that the recovery can be made.

For the sake of an analogy let us suppose a man became paralyzed as the result of traumatic shock in his youth. His inability to walk shielded him thereafter from anything resembling the original threat which occasioned the shock. No amount of anatomical or other objective knowledge concerning his body and no amount of observation of other's walking aroused him from his immobility. One night he had a very vivid dream, in which he was again a child, prancing about freely for no purpose at all. In the dream he remembered how *it felt to want to walk,* and when he awoke from the dream, he walked again.

The relationship between the aesthetic vision and practical living is analogous to that between the dream and the waking condition of this man. What the man dreamed was not that walking was better than not-walking, nor that his not being able to walk was an insidious enemy working from within him, but very simply what it really felt like to want to walk. It was not enough for him to "will to walk," for he somehow kept himself from "remembering"

how *really to will* this in his waking life. The recovery of spontaneity in art is much the same. The "dream" of art is nothing
more than a dream, but it stands ever as reminder to us of our
own capacity to be the original free makers of our self-in-its-world,
whether in dreams or in our waking involvements. The revolutionary aspect of such a dream consists not in that it proposes
revolt against, or changes of, anything, but in that it always holds
before us the possibility of choosing to be the freedom that we are,
and therefore of doing or undoing our self-in-our-life-world.

From this it follows that art as such carries no efficacy necessarily
in arousing men to change their world. It is the men themselves
who carry this potential impulse as something latent in themselves,
something waiting to be sprung into action. But, more commonly,
it is repressed or profoundly submerged. The revolutionary character of all art springs into being, therefore, when the aesthetic
presence is enacted by the man who has some awareness of his
own paralytic condition, so to speak, and has some willingness to
walk again. But there is also a significant sense in which such
enactment cannot but have effect—positive or negative—on every
kind of man.

Negative or reactionary rebellious effect consists in this, that the
aesthetic enactment stirs up the dread of being one's own freedom
in the man who fears to be himself. Even such a man, however,
must be capable of the enactment to some degree before this can
happen or, let us say, must be capable of enough of an entrance
into the enactment to remember what it is like to be the freedom
which he shuns and fights in his own being. (The man totally
lacking in capacity to feel and to imagine would not be a man at
all.) Reaction against aesthetic invitation to renew spontaneity can
take different forms. There is the man who when confronted by the
work of art takes aggressive cover under self-righteous moralizing,
preaching its "danger" to public morals. There is the man who
reacts by neutralizing the effect on him by an effort at ridicule.
And there is the man who quickly reaches for the "truth" in some
version or other, to convince himself and others that what he sees
cannot be (such a man, incidentally, ought really to argue that the
work of art is not "visible" in any and all senses of the word!).

Provided this is seriously taken into account, it would not be
improper to say that *The Stranger* "expresses revolt against the
value-schemes and institutions of twentieth century European man;
it tells the story of the reduction of this man to a meaningless

thing, tossed aimlessly on a sea of absurdity; and there is little more left for such a man if he would give any meaning to his existence, than to live in the sensuous moment, face and accept the absurd in its finality of death, and send to hell all supernatural palliatives on which his culture has been nursed." Fundamental condition for the propriety of such a statement is that one who makes it must *not* proclaim it as the "truth" about *The Stranger.* There is no "truth" to art; art can only be *truthful.*

And it is precisely this truthfulness of the authentic work of art which makes it the very embodiment of the revolutionary spirit. Like the child who speaks his mind without malice, telling the truth among stiffened, formal, and hypocritical lying adults, art stands ever ready to deflate and to expose all our studied pretenses. For what it "opposes," "confirms," "ridicules," "condemns," or "approves"—when it "does" any of these things—is the shape and form that man himself gives himself, and not merely certain causes and issues divorced from human purposing. When it incites men to rebel, the rebellion is radical, reaching to the very depths of his being, since there is nothing more fundamental and basic to our lives than sincerity of feeling, and art is the only way we have of maintaining such effective cleanliness or sincerity at its source.

What has so far been said would be of little worth in aesthetics if it did not apply also to art works which seem to have little or nothing to do with criticism of man and his values. Within the above indicated understanding of "revolutionary" and "rebellious," all art is revolutionary and rebellious in character. For if, as we maintain, it is the purposing agent himself that it arouses out of his lethargy and passivity, then it can arouse this agent in any and all the active facets of his being. It is well to remember that aesthetic purposing makes the actuality of all the realities of man's experience, and not merely that in which his political and economic interests find their near presence and urgency. Thus, *perception* itself, whether visual, auditory, or tactile, understood as the work of purposive activity, is ever renewable by the enactments of art.

Consider what Matisse's *Odalisque rouge* actualizes, in the first place, as a way of seeing anything and everything, or of "making" felt visual perceptions generally. Matisse himself said that he intends his art to do no more than relax the tired working man at the end of his day's labor. The *Odalisque,* in fact, offers this relaxed vision wherein the world appears not only in its undisguised sensuousness, but also relaxed in the way that practiced and familiar lovers are relaxed when they approach one another in embrace. There is here no tightness of effort, no inhibition, no formality. The elements produce a sensual, luxuriant richness which, by design, is deliciously lacking in ponderous depth. If anything remains hidden, it is only the secrecy and mystery of the harem, whose promises are already familiar in their quality. This is a world that is and is intended to be nothing else but surface play; it is a world in which form is impressed upon things with imperceptible, spontaneous effort. There is a sense of "waiting for something to happen," just because nothing is happening to draw our attention. Yet whatever is to happen carries no anxieties, no alert to action. Color values are at their lowest, hues are high-pitched. The world hangs together by a repetition which balances complementation with contrast in rich varieties, but the excitement announces only quiet harmony of delight in sensual variation. What passion is on display is a casual one, issuing from no subterranean intellectual depths, but from the body alone. One here looks upon the world without too much effort or concentration, but what he sees is vivid and entertainingly varied and complex. Such a world almost risks being simple decoration, but even this risk delights.

The whole of this way of feeling is cast in an image suggestive of a reclining female figure amidst surroundings which speak for quiet retirement and sensuous pleasure. This is the image-equivalent of the feeling. Luxuriant and mysteriously inviting to sensuous delights, this is a world far removed from the conflicts of the world of action. Heavily though colorfully curtained against the outside world, this environment is, though a kind of prison, nevertheless a beguiling and tempting one. It is a world of flesh, intoxicating perfumes, and sinuous, orgasmic movements. This is a place where the forbidden can be tasted without fear of being taken by surprise. Here one can let oneself go in unguarded and somehow allowable carnal confession.

What is there so revolutionary about such possibility of seeing, feeling, and doing? Well, for one thing, the Judeo-Christian tradition has so inculcated the condemnation of such possibility in Western man, that spontaneous sensuality presents the very face of Satan to the average individual. Even the man not particularly equipped with "morals" guards himself to keep honest desire from having free play. With all too many of us, the recognition, acceptance, and joyful enactment of such desires require an inner battle of such proportions that victory over oneself is often little more than a Pyrrhic victory, entailing feelings of guilt that must of necessity cripple any capacity for repetition of spontaneous acts. A man must come out from hiding in order to re-enact himself in spontaneity of this sort.

Of course, Matisse's *Odalisque rouge* no more invites men to seek the pleasures of the harem, than Camus' *The Stranger* invites them to be unloving to their mothers, kill Arabs, or reject the belief in an afterlife.

In Matisse, the feelings and the images are still, as we say, "recognizable." But what can be said about any one of the great collection of works known as "non-objectivist" painting including everything done since the French Cubists? To speak of this significantly, one would have to address himself to each work in the unique enactment of a possibility of feeling and imagining which it presents. Some things can be said, however, which apply generally to these works.

In the first place, none of the works in question are such, in their constitutive elements and in the manner of the composition of their elements, as to be so unrecognizable that no one can enact them as possibilities of feeling and imagining. Lines are lines, colors are colors, feelings are feelings, and images are images, no matter where one encounters them. The same can be said of any ordering of these. The elements and their orderings are the same in art as in ordinary experience. We have to be in possession of wholes of imaged feelings or felt images to have any experiences whatsoever. In art, these same elements and their organic orderings are made and sustained in actuality independently of the whole of that engaged-project which we know as wakeful reality and life. The fact that they are thus held in an actuality which does not mix with the "real" one does not annul their pertinence to that reality. In the aesthetic vision, we lift out and hold in an actuality all their own the elemental "materials" out of which experiential reality is made, and for no other purpose than to make, order, and present them in their pure possibility of being, and to make and present a pure possibility of being-our-self in it at the same time. The artist is under no restrictions as to *how* the world must be put together and for *whom*. Most important of all, the elements and their organization are never abstractions, but concrete actuality. Sometimes the artist chooses to build his world so that these elements and their orderings speak for the spontaneous purposing which makes, simply, elements and their orderings. And this is what a thoroughly "abstract" or "non-objective" work of art is. In this sense, it would be more correct to say that all art is essentially non-objective. It would take little search to find evidences of this kind of art in every epoch and in every culture—particularly when reputed conceptions of human knowledge fall into disrepute or when religious, scientific or philosophical concerns shake the foundations of accepted beliefs regarding "reality." Art sometimes mirrors the old and sometimes, in its own way, advances the new being behind the appearance which is losing credibility and ground. We must discern this dual role of abstract art.

It is obvious that the "non-objective" artist in our time is performing an operation on perceiving itself, which parallels the dissection and re-orientation of human knowledge gained in science and philosophy at least since Galileo established the existence of the moons of Jupiter, demolishing the Medieval crystalline spheres. "Optical reality" of previous days is everywhere challenged—not just in art, but also, and above all, in the affairs of the world. The atom bomb exploded in the works of many early French artists of the modern period even before it exploded in the American desert; and it is already exploding in world-wide holocaust in the work of some painters, even before modern nihilist man accomplishes the insane feat. The dismemberment of the Spanish man in Picasso's *Guernica,* so fundamentally pertinent to a fuller range of human values, has its parallel, so far as optical actuality goes, in the dismemberment of a bottle, or a chair, in a modern abstract still-life. It is not, moreover, dismemberment and explosion alone that we see in non-objective art, but new synthesis and new ways of perceiving as well.

Earlier, we mentioned Italian Futurist creations as "speaking the first word" concerning a world in motion, streamlined for speed. Much of modern non-objective art first uttered the realities of contemporary existing man; much of it uttered also the last, recapitulating word; and still another part did both together.

Paul Cézanne's reconstruction of perceptual sensitivity was far-reaching in its effects, not only upon art, but on perceptual sensitivity in general. The sense of structure and the making of value-gradations in and through hues and intensities of color was rediscovered: this, after a long period during which, both in and out of the museum, perception had lost its vision, so to speak, and its depth and gradations had been reduced to an absence rather

than a presence of color. Human perception had been intellectual-
ized into an atrophied, conventionalized product, where vital structure and vibrant actuality were lost. Cézanne introduced an
extraordinarily clear and simple vision, a naïveté of sensibility
which freshened up the world of visual perception. It was this return to direct vision, this de-intellectualization of perception which
held in embryo nearly every later development of modern art. This
vitalization has passed into our ordinary ways of perceiving things
—from advertising to the building of functional structures.

No small part of this renewal of spontaneity in perceiving was
the implicit self-recovery of the maker himself of perception, the
agency behind the perception. The phenomenon of this recovery
we first see unfolding in the work of the French *Fauves* and the
whole Expressionist movement to this day. On the side of the renewed sense of structure and of the revitalization in color, the
heirs of Cézanne were the Impressionists and the Cubists respectively. If we mention the Expressionists first, it is because this was,
and had naturally to be, the more existentially significant, more
hazardous, and more persistent extension. The work of Cézanne
himself would, at first view, appear to show little of the expressionist
or personal engagement with his new-found vision, but this is deceiving. First, the new vision itself which he put forth comes with
the man, and second, his very lack and failure, when it comes to
"speaking" more than or beyond structure and color, reveal in their
very pathos the presence of a self seeking for itself.[84]

Modern expressionism in its enormous proliferation has been—
and still is—the noisy, seething experimental laboratory for Western
man's aesthetic models for selfhood in a world in which the older
patterns have been discredited. It has tried everything, sometimes
borrowing from the latest current of thought and fashion, and
sometimes striking out on its own. It has tried its hand at models of
selfhood and of perception drawn from Marx, from Freud, from
African sculpture, from classical statuary, from the machine, and
from a thousand other sources. Often, this frantic search and ex-
perimentation has reached what would seem ridiculous proportions.
There are artists who in the name of art have a model randomly
wriggle on a paint-smeared canvas, or even seek to produce art with
absolute automatism, by means of gadgets, with a minimum of in-
tervention by the human being. Even a "painting machine" has been
invented! Needless to say, as a phenomenon revealing of the human

[84] His timidity with the nude is well known.

condition, such excesses, if excesses they be, are nothing to laugh about.

As mirror and recapitulator of life, modern art has exhibited a great variety of interpretations of the outcome and condition of Western man and his civilization. Modern art was first to put on exhibit the nihilism, the vacuity, the despair, and the deathly mechanization and depersonification of the existing man in our time.[85] One has to have experienced what Sartre calls "nausea" to know the honesty of certain modern expressions. In much of this art, there is all the explosion, the dismemberment of the human soul, and the distortion which anyone who cares to look, can easily find in our troubled world. If in this art the object of perception and the whole world of such objects have fallen apart in violence, so also has the mind and soul of modern man.

That both novel projections and retrospective commentaries are one thing in art, and quite a different thing in real life, bears emphatic repetition if we would understand the sense in which art can be said to be revolutionary in character. The being of the work of art is a concrete enactment of a possibility as such, and not merely a thing or a thing-event. In real life, dismemberment and distortion appear as disorder from which we would flee; novel projections of purpose often seem disruptive and dangerous—as disorder of another kind. In art, where the purposing-at-work is form-giving or ordering *par excellence,* disorder itself becomes the very possibility of a way of ordering. And it is precisely because this possibility can be enacted, that the disorder can clearly be seen, looked at, and intimately felt and imagined.

This power of art is a power to show with limpid clarity what things and men can be, or what they have become, without intent to do anything else. Men can be shown, or show themselves, some thing or some course of action without necessarily having to become stirred or moved in their will to act in any way. Or they may be deeply affected by what is shown, especially when what is shown is a vital reminder of themselves in some role which they would act on, or have some sense of shame of playing or of having played. But in real life all "showing," in the sense here intended, comes already loaded with suggestions for action; we show in order to buy, sell, exchange, ridicule, protest, and in a thousand other ways arouse ourselves and one another to action. Aesthetic vision does

[85] Paul Tillich, *The Courage to Be* (New Haven: Yale University Press, 1952), pp. 142-148.

not come so loaded. If it arouses us in any practical way, it is because it finds us ready, one way or another, to act. Not the works of art, therefore, but the man himself carries in his being the potential of rebellion and revolution. If we say of art that it is rebellious and revolutionary, it is because it represents our most fundamental impulse to be honest about ourselves and about our world. And it is this that warrants our saying that art is the most revolutionary thing there is.

Existing men can be divided into several kinds. There are those who secretly or overtly are running away in panic from what they have been and done, without direction and knowledge of what they want to be or do. There are those who, by devious ways, have convinced themselves that they can find their meaning in the repetition of their former or present roles, resisting to the death any change. There are those who somehow succeed in entering a state of self-oblivion or insensitivity, remaining immobilized in indifference and passivity, suffering external changes not of their own initiation. Finally, there are those who, having come to the realization that there is no fulfillment in the past or the present, cautiously open themselves to the envisionment of new possibilities.

For the first three kinds of men, it is more than likely that the aesthetic enactment will be abortive, and its effects on the enactor will do more harm than good. But, because this assertion can be no more than a generalization from observed cases, the possibility cannot be excluded that even here art can sometimes bestir the enactor into self-concern. More often than not, however, the first kind of man responds to the aesthetic vision as to a refuge from his flight, postponing thereby the day of existential decision, and taking its invitation to be his own spontaneous self as an invitation to pseudo-bohemian irresponsibility in living. The aesthetic enactment may fill the second class of man with resentment and revolt at the very sight of the possibility of being which appears to question his own entrenched position. For the third kind, art can be no more than an opiate to keep his pleasant state of sleep undisturbed. It is only for the fourth kind of man that the aesthetic enactment can be truly self-liberating and constructive in its renovating effects.

Though there is no good or bad art in the moral sense of the word, and although no authentic work of art ever enters the world of human contentiousness, perhaps we can now see how it is that art can, in its effects on certain kinds of men, be good or bad for them depending on their inward condition. In my opinion, this is something that Plato understood very well, and that his interpreters and translators have all too often failed to see. It remains true, however, that Plato had settled for an unchangeable Good which aesthetic vision could only help reveal to men growing from *Eros* into *Agape,* in their capacity to Love; art did not, for Plato, enter into the actual creation of the good. The thoroughgoing existentialist position we are here taking permits us to say that poetry is truly ontological *poesis* or making—it brings the very possibility of being into actual being, showing it as such, whether men work on it or not in their lives, and however they may take it in such work. Nor must we disown the full implications of this position for ethics. For this reason, it becomes appropriate to mention one such important implication in passing.

The connection between the "is" and the "ought," the descriptive and the normative, the fact and the value, has ever been a puzzle in philosophy. Much has been written on the subject, yet little if any headway has been made. In more recent times, the puzzlement and confusion have been aggravated by the now unbridgeable disparity between what science says are the facts about the world (including man), and what religion, especially in its more orthodox forms, says they are. For a time, at the end of the nineteenth century, an intense and vociferous debate developed around this question. The very inconclusiveness of the debate, as well as that fake tolerance and hypocritical piousness among men which counsel prudential silence, eventually brought an uneasy peace. At present, the parties concerned, for their private interests, with the implications of any given solution to the problem have all learned the difficult and rather remarkable technique of saying what one does not mean and meaning what one does not say. This includes understanding what one's opponent does not understand, and not understanding what the other understands very well. This verbal and intellectual prestidigitation is particularly in evidence in philosophical literature where, under the convenient guise of great intellectual modesty and humility, we have learned to be very minute about very minute parts of very large issues, secretly hoping that such minutiae will resolve these same large issues without the trouble and risk of having to acknowledge their existence and importance. A man caught with certain implications of his limited statements about certain other limited statements, will quickly disown the entire enterprise by assuring you that he "is speaking, really, only to a very special and confined point." The curious thing about this is that we have even come to identify such pusillanimous trickery with professional dignity and scholarship!

Between what is, and what ought to be, there can be no inert relation, such as logicians and physical scientists have to deal in for their very special purposes. As a matter of fact, there can be no relation at all, if one means by this some "objective" connection which is not the existing man himself who relates them by choice, commitment, and existential decision. For whatever is, is; but what ought to be, can only be what some existent desires, wants, hopes, or dreams that he might somehow bring into being. What causes the trouble in discussions of this problem is invariably the presuppositions regarding the status in being, the ontological status of this "what" in "what somebody desires, wants, hopes, or dreams for." And the presuppositions are forever being patterned after the abstractions that mathematicians, natural scientists, and other "objective" inquirers have to invent and agree upon in order to expedite their own work.

The "what" in "what I ought to do" refers, in every case, both to a resolve or decision not yet made, and to some self-role-in-my-life-world somehow pre-figured or known before its enactment. The decision and the role cannot be separated, for they are aspects of one and the same thing, and together can have their actual being only in the enactment. If we ask, how can such a thing be pre-figured, known beforehand, laid out before it happens, we raise a very important question—the most important in ethics, perhaps. The abstractionist-intellectualist in ethics has no difficulty in replying to this question nor, for that matter, does his opponent, the positivist, for whom the enactment in question is a matter of action on the basis of desire and emotion. The first makes the "ought" into an "is" of what is called "Reason," logically deducible from such, and the second makes it into an "is" of description, generalizable from observed fact. The first says: "This is what men ought to do because this is what Reason says they are," and the second says: "This is what men *do* do, and that is all that can be said about it." Both of these positions practice reduction of the "ought" into a *thing,* a thing or object of the abstracting mind, and a thing or object of description, respectively. Implicit in both reductions there is reification of man-in-his-life-world.

When philosophizing is pursued as a quest for concreteness, all abstractionist reductions and reifications are shunned. Here it is understood that, torn asunder, or held apart, or reduced one to the other, "is" and "ought" can be only interested contrivances which serve in projects where, what a man is, and what he ought to be and do are matters already settled upon—programs in process of being carried out.

Concretely speaking, an existing man never is what he is, and in two different senses of the expression: he is now no longer what he made of himself, and not yet what he will make himself if he takes another breath and makes another decision. That any man can act without involving himself in the making and the enacting of new self is a fiction: one who chooses to eat a steak chooses also to be that particular steak-eater, and one who chooses to dictate makes himself into a dictator. Again, the existing man always is what he is not, which means that he is neither what he has already made of himself, nor what he has not yet made of himself through action. Taken together, these characteristics provide us with the precise background against which the "what" in "what I ought to do" can properly be discussed. And the first thing that must be said is in the nature of a paradox: this "what" is something, and nothing. For, when I say "I ought or ought not do such and such to my friend Joe," I certainly am referring to a certain program of *my* possible actions which I know I have not yet realized into action. I know also that this program is such that, even if I never acted upon it, I could still at least bring it before consciousness as an enactment of purpose which was never acted upon.

The problem is to determine what this prefigurement can possibly be, which may enter bodily into my passing from my "is" as a self-in-its-life-world, to my "ought" as another-yet-the-same-self-in-its-life-world. The passing or execution itself of the enactment obviously engages the whole of myself as purposing agent, under that posture of my being which I call deciding, choosing to be, or becoming myself (more exactly, making myself into myself).

Anybody who observes himself carefully, and who reports on himself honestly will admit that there is no irresistible power and thrust, either in abstract intellectual prefigurations, or in the description of event-facts as such. When it appears to me in reflection that my doing or not doing such and such to my friend Joe was impelled by some piece of deductive reasoning, or by consideration of my own or other's observable behavior, it is certain that I have aborted my report of my own doings, or was unable to reach to their depths. It takes, however, no involved psychoanalysis, and no amount of any other kind of special knowledge for me to understand that, no matter what part descriptions and intellectualizations may have played in the situation, the convincingness of a certain sincerely felt-imagined possibility of my being-myself in a certain role, played in its correlative world, had more to do with "making up my mind" than anything else. It is true that this, as any other such possibility, could have been enacted by me without its necessarily arousing me to do or not to do what I did to my friend, but it happened that the enactment of this particular possibility found me, as a whole man, in that condition and situation where it had the effect that it did. There is no difference in kind, between those possibilities which I may have enacted in feeling and imagination, but on which I did not act, and this on which I did act.

The idea that aesthetic purposing is the only bridge between fact and value is an old one, one to which, in one form or another, philosophers seem ever to return after long and fruitless excursions into the abstractions of both reason and empiricistic thinking. Immanuel Kant tried to make it the pivot of his great philosophical account of experienced human reality.[86] What has prevented the theory from coinciding with truth about concreteness, however, is that the aesthetic was seen either as directly, or by its own hand, effecting the connection between fact and value, or else as representing a confused and unautonomous stage or degree of Reason. My position here is that it is the whole purposing being who picks up his aesthetic envisionments in order to enact his "oughts," and that aesthetic purposing has its own *raison d'être* and justification. The power that art has for man's moral improvement resides in the fact that both aesthetic and moral purposing are, after all, facets of the single existent, and the further fact that aesthetic purposing is the font and source of all honesty and sincerity.

The reader will no doubt have noticed that we feel no need to take precautions against the fact that art can and often does lend itself also to the hidden purposes of the first three kinds of men listed above.[87] Do we, then, make of art something neutral and indifferent to the condition of man, available to the free and the unfree alike? Yes, this can be said to be what we are doing, provided one knows also that freedom is not something like a ladder, by which some object called "The Good" is reached, but the good itself for man; and provided, also, that he knows unfreedom to be

[86] In the *Critique of Judgment*.
[87] See page 131.

the living essence of evil for man. The freedom that is art, and the freedom that existing man would be and needs to be, meet only in existential commitment and decision, where the free act of art becomes one with action or with life itself. In short, the idea that something which in itself has nothing to do with either good or evil can enter substantially into the very formation of the good man and the good world, should be troublesome only to those for whom the good man and the good world are no open and free projects, but exclusive institutionalized interests to be pitted against one another.

Conceptions of the beautiful specifically designed to accord with exclusive and preferred views of the good and the true, may be interesting articles to know about and to examine for whatever is in them, but what they are in terms of human purposive doings has to be dug out, for it is never evident on the surface.

The history of the moral renovation and improvement of human life through aesthetic vision has never been written. Those among the philosophers who suspected some connection between art and morality, invariably proceeded to construct aesthetic theories which made of art a handmaiden of moralities already delivered and lived out. But making of art a pedagogical tool is no way of recognizing and affirming its service to morality. For art's relation to morality is such that, more often than not, rather than giving fresh life to dead moralities, it helps deliver new ones against the old.

The Poet-Philosopher is more articulate on this problem than we could ever be:

O my brethren! With whom lieth the greatest danger to the whole human future? Is it not with the "good" and the "just"?

As those who say and feel in their hearts: "We already know what is good and just, we possess it also; woe to those who still seek thereafter!"

And whatever harm the wicked may do, the harm of the "good" is the harmfulest harm!

O my brethren, into the hearts of the good and just looked someone once upon a time, who said: "They are the Pharisees." But people did not understand him . . . (Friedrich Nietzsche, *Thus Spake Zarathustra*).

CHAPTER FIVE

Art & the Record of Art

PHENOMENOLOGY OF THE *THING*

We return now to the thing we sometimes call the physical work of art. The first observation we must make is that, all appearances to the contrary, this is really the most difficult object to locate and to discern. No small part of this difficulty resides in our incorrigible habit of confusing concrete things with abstractions.

If there is a "physical" side to the work of art, this, too, must be an item in that life-world which is the only concrete and experiential world we know. What is not concrete in this sense is abstraction, something instituted and maintained in being by thought alone. Fundamental existential understanding consists, above all else, in understanding the purposes for such contrivances (though, of course, their structures can be described phenomenologically also). But what we must concern ourselves with here is the concrete thing, our main object being to show that the art-*thing* which truly has to do with art is in the nature of a *directive record* which helps us determine the *locus* of the enactment which is art, and, also, affords us, in a certain way, the power-to-act-out the enactment. For this purpose, we must begin with a few observations concerning the model of all concrete *things;* namely, our own bodies.

The thing I know as my concrete body at the moment that I am writing might be described something as follows: the purposing effort that I myself am comes structured in such a way that its activity is bounded, at any particular moment, by limits of power-to-enact-itself, and by absence or failure of such power. What this potency and lack of potency are I know intimately in the act in which I attempt any kind of action. My intent and decision to move my arms and hands in order to hit the typewriter keys to write down my ideas, for example, easily and quickly become translated into action, so that my purposive effort becomes not only explicated into, but fixed, at a certain place, in my life-world, as part of that world. On the other hand, there are some intentions and decisions which I cannot so explicate and fix. I cannot, for example, now and in this particular situation shake hands with my friend Fred, who is in another city, or even converse with him on the ideas I am trying to put down without at least picking up the phone. Moreover, some things I am permitted to do with such ease that I hardly notice any difference or separation between my purposive effort, and the available power-to-act which enters into its embodiment, whereas, some other things I can do only against a certain resistance or impairment of such power. Thus, I am hardly aware of moving my arm as I type; but if I should shift the position of my body to the left, and then turn its upper part ever so slightly to the right, my stretched spinal ligament would immediately announce pain and inability to act. Some power-to-act, like the power to liquidate, without moving a finger, the annoying mosquito which is buzzing around me, is not available to me at all.

Concretely considered, my body is precisely this structured potency and lack of potency, this particular present empowerment of my purposing being located always at some particular place, at a particular time. I have an intimate acquaintance with it, a *knowledge* of it which differs in kind from any biological, physiological, or other scientific kind that I may have of it. (Much that I think I know about, in these other ways, in fact, corresponds to nothing that I can know concretely, or in this same actual and intimate way.) But it must not be thought that this structured-available-potency which I call my "body" is, concretely speaking, anything beyond what fully appears to me in the acts in which I try to empower my intentions and my choices: neither my body nor any other can be a power-to-act-in-general. All of which, of course, has nothing to say about the nature, worth, and value of any intellectual or other constructions which I might set up by way of scientific or other hypothesizing regarding my body. We do not concern ourselves now with such constructions except to say, in passing, that we see them as instrumental extensions of body or power-to-act in the concrete sense.

From the above, it may be understood that the thing I call my body is not a *thing* at all in the ordinary sense, but a limited and particular availability, simply, of capacity and power to act which is my very own. To the question, "What is it like to be my body?" the answer is that to be my body is to be able to act in the particular ways I do act, including not being able to act in certain other ways. But if by "body" is meant, not my body, or any other living body, but a thing, say, like the "physical" object we refer to as Brancusi's *Bird in Flight,* our question would, at first view, seem inappropriate and even meaningless. It would seem like asking "What is it like to be a piece of brass?"

Would it really be meaningless to ask this last question? Are there circumstances under which it would be, rather, most significant and important?

The concrete account of my bodily existence involves a most intimate account of all my life-actions—the full account of an inward unfolding history of actions, feelings, images. Some might say that such account could be only in the nature of an introspective psychological report of little more than personal, autobiographical value only. It so happens, however, that psychological introspections properly speaking have always been on the order of "objective" undertakings of a certain kind of inquiry, hence scientific and excluded from our present concerns. From the standpoint of objectivity in inquiry, it makes no difference in principle whether the "data" observed consist of happenings occurring in consciousness or outside of consciousness. The concrete, as we here understand it, is neither in nor outside consciousness; it is neither subjective, nor objective, but a reality prior to any such dissections performed for whatever purposes they are performed.

In order significantly to address the question about concrete being to Brancusi's *Bird in Flight,* insofar as this is taken as a concrete body or thing, we must be able to ask it in the same way that I asked the question about my concrete bodily existence. How can this be done? How, that is, can we seriously look upon such an inert and unfeeling object as the empowerment of purposing in the same way that I certainly can do with what I call my body? For is it not just a lump of brass, albeit externally shaped in a certain way by a purposing agent called Brancusi? Our problem must not be one of projecting or proposing strange and unusual ways of considering the thing before us but, strange as it may seem, the most obvious, the most common, the most direct way of considering it.

If elsewhere we reminded the reader that obviousness conceals things, here the reminder is doubly necessary. The moment we project the question, What is it?—referring to the naked concrete thing as thing—everybody, and particularly the grave scholar, entirely forgets his customary and natural way of considering it. The very question seems to change the thing to which it is addressed into an entirely different object. Thus, for example, we tend to put aside Brancusi's personal purposive effort as well as our own in shaping the *Bird in Flight* as something irrelevant to the thing we are observing—we suddenly become physicists, chemists, metallurgists, what-not, as if such postures in purposing were the only ones possible to give sense to our question.

The truth of the matter is that the questions, "What is the *thing*, Brancusi's *Bird in Flight*?" and, "What sort of unique enactment does it relate to?" cannot be separated, even as in our ordinary and actual encounter with this art work we do not in fact separate them. Of course, we do and must separate them when we deliberately are operating as physicists, or in some other such way, but this is another matter altogether. What we wish to understand is what *this thing* is which finds its actuality in the total reality of Brancusi's *Bird in Flight* when it is this art work that we purpose to understand. Outside of the aesthetic concern, any knowledge we might care to seek of such object is irrelevant to our understanding of the art work as art work. But we had better try and say what we have to say about this concrete *thing* before us, in the very same way that we spoke of "my body."

Imagine that I do what I call "taking myself to the exact spot where Brancusi's piece is now on public exhibit," in order to do what I call seeing his *Bird in Flight*, after which I stand before it. My determining to go to the spot, and to place what I call my body into intimate contact with the object is no matter extraneous to our account. It is possible for me to take my body to that same spot, before the same object, in order to expedite any number of other purposes having nothing whatsoever to do with aesthetic enactments. One who sees Brancusi's *Bird in Flight* obviously has undertaken to do so, even if this involves no more than to turn his eyes to it. The point is that one must attend to such a thing as one must attend to any other life-project. Were Brancusi's statue

placed before me, I would still have to move or act in order to
attend to it in that very special kind of way which is called for, no
matter how imperceptible my action. This is the sense in which the
world does not come to me: I go to it, even when it crashes on my
head. This must be said because, concretely speaking, my encounter
with the world or any of its concrete items is always a unique and
particular one, in which I enact the purposing that I am in particular ways. If there are times and occasions when my encounter
is so feebly interested or engaged that the world appears as a moving
shadow, I may be on the very verge of sleep, but even then whatever vision I still have of it is sustained and gradually dissolved in
the relaxation of my purposing activities.

But it is not entirely correct to say, though I just did, that the
world never comes to me. What I should have said is that it never
comes to me in the same way that I go to it, or attend to it. It
shows up, first of all, in that particular and special *field* that I know
as my body, concretely understood; and it shows up as a sort of
extension of that same body, in the form of its own availabilities,
impairments, or absolute negations of power-to-act. Only in this
sense does it intrude upon me, or confront me, as something other
than my own body. Thus, before I attended to Brancusi's sculpture,
I had no way of being able to enact the aesthetic work, but now
that I have attended to it, and am in fact before it, this power or
capacity is added on to my own. But, it does not appear that my
attending to, my exposing myself to the object is sufficient to afford
me this expansion of my power-to-act. I might, conceivably, take
myself to the exhibit, stand before the sculpture, yet fail utterly
to appropriate it in the way just indicated; or I might be able to
appropriate it only to a certain extent (which is what more often
is apt to happen). There thus arises the interesting question of
what exactly is it that shows up in the concrete world of my bodily
existence under these possibilities, and it is this question that we
must pursue in earnest, if we would understand the nature of the
thing we are trying to observe in its essential concrete *thingness*.

Suppose I now stand before Brancusi's piece yet am unable to
see it, in the sense explained throughout this book. I see something,
of course, in the ordinary sense of having some visual, kinaesthetic,
and other impressions, which means that power-to-act other non-
aesthetic projects is afforded me by my encounter with the thing.
The very least of these projects is what might be called, "an indeterminate object found placed on a pedestal at such and such

an art museum, in such and such a room and spot in that room, in the midst of paintings and sculptures" (assuming that the other objects in the room presented me with no difficulties in enacting aesthetic objects). Other less probable but available possibilities might be: "something of a certain weight and shape to be thrown against one who is attacking me"; "a piece of metal which can be melted down and remolded into useful objects"; "an object which, when looked at, is responded to by certain people in such and such ways." The list of such possibilities, whether improbable or not under the circumstances, would, in any case, be limited. Normally, it would be impossible for me to see the thing as "something with which, if one wanted to, one could go to the moon," or "an object I am now dreaming." The point we are trying to make is that the recalcitrance to my intent to enact an aesthetic object, even when my own incapacity to so enact is granted, is never absolutely nothing. For this to happen, I would have to be unable to see anything at all, and be confirmed in my experience by other beings with whom I share the fundamental project of acting, feeling, and perceiving itself.

Although this is a far-reaching question which does not directly concern us here, we must ask whether or not we can say that the thing, in its concrete thingness, is the totality, simply, of all the possible projects for which it could provide power of enactment to purposing beings. Such assertion could, of course, itself be nothing other than the conclusion of an extremely recondite project, namely, "making a coherent system of ideas or thoughts in which, ideally, concrete things as such are accounted for metaphysically." We must distinguish such a project from the one at hand, which is to describe the phenomenon of the concrete thing as far as we can without resort to abstractions of any kind. From the point of view of a phenomenological description, it appears certain that, over and beyond all the possibilities as power-to-act, the thing has a certain residuum of being which cannot be easily resolved into pure possibility of action. For, apart from the fact that the total of such possibilities is always and in every case limited, the possibilities themselves are not of the order, say, of the kind presented by aesthetic purposing as works of art. They are "real" possibilities for action in the waking-state life-world of men. In short, the power-to-act enjoys a persistence and endurance all its own, and in some sense, it stands independent of all the empowerings of purposes to which it can lend itself. Phenomenologically speaking, this constitutes that *ob-jecting* characteristic of every real object that our purposing being encounters, when it confronts anything which truly does not resolve into our own kind of being. We are referring to a concrete impact, and not to any theory about such. Thus, if I, in the illustration, could exhaust all the possibilities with respect to the thing which is not helping me to enact Brancusi's *Bird in Flight*, I would still, after consideration of each and all possibilities, find myself facing something foreign standing in my way, and seriously obstructing any wish I might have to make.

This helps us narrow down the concrete and existential sense of the *thing* in the illustration. Whether or not I bring to the thing any capacity to enact the *Bird in Flight* in the aesthetic sense, something is *there* which we should be able to identify for what it is—not, indeed, as some Kantian *Ding an Sich,* or metaphysical absolute—but as a concrete existential being entirely within the context of my purposing in going to "see" Brancusi's *Bird in Flight*. In order to proceed with the illustration, I have to assume a good many things, but none I could not check on, as it were. Thus, I assume that the thing before me was put together by some person; the actions of this person should be traceable to some extent on the very face of this thing; the thing has been handled in certain par-ticular ways, rather than in others (the appearance alone tells me this); obviously, whatever the material was, before it was so shaped, *somebody* selected it out of all that was available, and, even if nothing else was available, I know that it was *chosen* for this pur-pose. In my own way, I can re-enact for myself a whole series of actions required or called for, so far as I can see, to come to pro-duce such a shape from such material. Now my own bodily motions, together with their corresponding kinaesthetic accompaniments, come sympathetically and empathically into play. It is, in fact, with such internal *live* sense of my own body—the *thing* that I myself am—that I begin to "see" the thing which stands before me. But, of course, I have already crossed the line between the obscure, unyielding, positively dumb thing as it first confronted me, and what we have earlier called "elements" and "orderings of elements." A world of transparent qualities is now emerging "in" and "outside" my concrete bodily being, gradually supplanting what was there obscurely "given" to me earlier.

Where exactly did this new, this art-thing, begin to form, and how? More important to our present purposes, what, now, can be made of the connection between the "given" and the new formation?

I began this process of "seeing" at a point where my own living body became activated in a way whose order and progress were not only suggested by the shape and characteristics of the thing, but which, in some sense, remain actually and permanently inscribed in the thing. The art-thing *directs,* somehow, my enactment. It suggests and directs it in the way that the actual "physical" scribbles of, say, an old and familiar love note can suggest and direct the awakening of personal memories. The analogy is apt, because it indicates that it is my own self-disarming sincere and active receptivity, as well as something in the conformation of the thing insofar as it is a record of another's aesthetic enactment, that must enter into our account. The worst possible account would be to think of the enactment in the terms of a "stimulus-response" situation. For, the truth of the matter is that, in order that the enactment can even begin, I must be capable of enacting the very stimulus to which I can respond. The thing is already, not *any* thing, but a very special kind of thing, as well as a particular thing, to which I have already accorded, by my very posture in purposing, the power to help me speak and to guide me in forming my very own words in speaking.

What is it about Brancusi's work (considered strictly in this context) which makes it, not only eminently efficacious in suggesting and directing this particular aesthetic enactment, but suited to aesthetic purposes in the first place? In terms strictly of *thing,* the work appears to be first a locus or "place" where the enactment *can be,* or *show* itself in the world of action, and, second, a kind of blueprint for its construction. But above all it is a *public,* and, therefore, "impersonal" source of power-to-enact the kind of possible personality or possible-self-in-its-life-world which is the aesthetic presence. Under this latter aspect, it is much like a specially constructed "battery" available to any who wishes to use it for turning his own "wheels." But all of this is not itself the aesthetic enactment in its living actuality, which can arise only as an existing individual appropriates the opportunity, remaining faithful, in his enactment of the aesthetic vision, to what the art-thing allows and does not allow him to do. The "direction" here is in the nature of a control—not, indeed, of the enactment as such (which happens nowhere else, and for nobody else than in and for the existing enactor in his-life-world), but of the *action* or practical purposing in which the enactor must engage if he would enter into his enactment.

A phenomenon relative to the art-thing thus considered is the reproducibility of this art-thing. Even with those art works which formerly could not be reproduced with exactitude, or at all, various gadgets like high fidelity, motion pictures, and television now make faithful reproduction possible. As a phenomenon, the reproducibility of the art-thing conclusively shows, in the first place, that the art-thing is not the same as the enactment: the enactment cannot be reproduced, or reproduced in the same way. It shows also that the art-thing is by its very nature a thing *for use,* and that the art-thing, like its reproductions, may or may not be adequate to the living enactment it attempts to record. But, above all, it proves that the recording of the aesthetic enactment is not necessary to the enactment itself. Except for the non-aesthetic interests of the collector and speculator, any near-perfect reproduction of a Cézanne (such are now mechanically possible) is as adequate as the original. With music and the literary arts, this is even more evident. In the novel, it is even possible to reproduce the art-thing by translation into other languages or into a movie.

The fact is that any thing or object can be taken in the way we have just taken Brancusi's piece. This is what happens when we appropriate anything in what we call "nature" as spring-board for aesthetic enactments. What distinguishes Brancusi's piece from, say, a flying bird in the sky, is that the locus, the direction, and the power for the aesthetic enactment is, most of the time, intellectually taken to be anonymously made or arranged. Careful consideration of what we really do when we have aesthetic experiences of nature, however, reveals that the anonymity of the thing, concretely considered, in no way differs from the thing specifically designed to serve in aesthetic enactments generally. Behind this anonymity, some Brancusi, some agency, always is felt: what philosophers have called the "teleological view" of things is implicit in, and a necessary part of any concrete context wherein aesthetic enactments can occur. The philosopher of the concrete may well suspect that the very notion of teleology, wherever used, derives originally from aesthetic purposing.

Taken outside the concrete context of aesthetic purposing, the art-thing we are considering shows no special markings whatsoever which would indicate its special efficacies in setting the locus, blue-printing, and affording the "neutral" power to enact aesthetic presences. No analysis of the metal could possibly reveal what makes Brancusi's piece the unique work of art that it is, nor would any mathematical study of proportions and relationships. Before a

masterpiece of sculpture, we may be tempted to ask: "What makes
a piece of stone immortal?" No piece of stone is ever art, let alone
immortal.

There are, therefore, three distinct ways of considering any *thing:*
concretely, as locus, as directive blueprint, and as available or public
power-to-act non-aesthetically; abstractly, in the context of the various scientific inquiries which never investigate, nor are designed to
investigate, the concrete as such; and, lastly, as the art-thing we have
been describing. Only the last of these is directly related to the
aesthetic. It is in this context that the physical work of art can
properly be studied and analyzed. But it must now be clear that
what is studied and analyzed is an organism of concrete elements
and their orderings which are already aesthetic in their very nature.
These elements and their orderings can be nothing else than felt-
imaged beings, at once both subjective and objective—though it
is best to say that they are a reality which is prior to any such
distinctions. But if we care to use such terms, the objectivity of the
elements and their orderings consists in that aesthetic purposing
provides the element of actuality in every other form or posture of
purposing, insofar as it has to do with concrete, objective realities.
Which is to say that, though in such a thing as Brancusi's piece, the
elements and their orderings are, as it were, picked up for the
special purpose of constructing a directive record and potential enactment of a work of art, they remain nonetheless ubiquitous and
present underneath the very texture of all our concrete experience.
The felt-imaged mass, volume, direction, and texture of Brancusi's
brass piece are the same as we might encounter in other concretely
experienced objects anywhere else, and so, are also the felt-imaged
flowing harmonies of their arrangement or composition. Only, in
Brancusi's piece, these "building-blocks," and their organic composition are put together as a directive record of a certain enactment of aesthetic actuality, and not as another object to serve, say,
to sit on, or to poke the fire. But who is to stop us from using *Bird
in Flight* as a paper-weight, or as something to show our neighbors
that we are rich and cultured? Better still, since its possible uses are
so many, can we say that there are bad and good uses? And in what
sense of "good" and "bad," and on what criteria?

It is the basic identity of the elements and orderings of the art
record with the elements and orderings in the concrete life-world
or *Lebenswelt* of existing men which makes it possible for the art-

thing to serve as it does in the enactment of the aesthetic presence. But it is the role which this object assumes in the total context of aesthetic purposing in the life-world that permits the lifting of these same elements and their orderings out of the region of things as they are present and available *qua* utensils or tools for the enactment of non-aesthetic projects in the life-world. When Brancusi's *Bird in Flight* was first brought into the United States from Europe, the customs agents levied a tax on it, considering it to be simply so much brass and not a work of art at all. The customs agents may have had the capacity to feel the unique flow of the lines, and, some of them, may even have enjoyed running their hands over the surface of this piece of brass. But they missed the purposing context in which alone the art object as art object could be determined.

It is the basic identity of the elements and orderings in the art record with those in the life-world which makes it significant and illuminating for us to examine and to analyze the art thing in the terms of and in the language which applies to existence and the real world. Thus we can speak significantly of "light" and "heavy" masses, "quiet" and "agitated" forms, "hard" and "soft" lines. This, finally, is what also permits the fusion of art with life, wherein the possible and the real self-in-its-world seem to live in one another.

Such view of the art-thing together with its components and composition has nothing to do with the abstraction we can make of the art object when we take it out of its proper context. It is then that our analyses lead us to speak of irrelevancies such as the arrangement of Dante's *Divine Comedy* by three's and nine's, as if it were some exercise in arithmetic, or the number of times a certain word is used, or the oddities of spelling in the original manuscript.

There is the same connection between the art-thing and the aesthetic enactment, as there is between what some semanticists call the "vehicle" (the original denotative sense and use of the word) and the "tenor" (the complex of connotations now made to refer to something else) of a metaphor. (Thus, for example, the word *warmth* ordinarily refers to certain feelings or sensations, but in "the warmth of his personality," the connotations alone are preserved, and made to disclose the characteristics of a certain kind of person.) Analyzing the art-thing as such, is much like examining and laying bare the array and order of the connotations as they play their new role freed from their original but still possible role in denotative speech.

ON THE USES OF ART

The aesthetic enactment or presence as such has, of course, no use. In itself, art has no use or purpose, simply because it is the work of a purposing whose form-giving effort is spent on its own act, in the renewal of spontaneity itself. This means not that we should or should not use art-things but, simply, that art as enactment is such that it cannot in any sense be used and that any attempt to do so must result in its non-enactment. On the other hand, the art-thing or record, independently considered, not only can be used but, in a special sense, cannot but be used.

The first and immediate use of the art-thing is as directive record for the particular aesthetic enactment. Thus considered, such record may or may not be so constructed as to effect this end properly. This is what we mean when, pointing to the work of art, we say that there is certainly something there, but something is wrong with the composition, or with something else: that the artist should improve his drawing and painting, the poet his vocabulary and grammar, the composer his harmony or counter-point, and so on. We are not saying that improved or different technique would in itself make or generate the art presence which has already begun to form, but that it would better direct and record the formation of such enactment. And this is the only sense in which it can properly be said that although the artist has fully enacted the art presence for himself, he has failed—because of some lack in his record—to help others do the same for themselves. Assuming that we can suppose the artist to have enacted the aesthetic presence for himself (something which, in any case, is indicated only by the fact that we perceive something in his work), the lack must not be thought of as lack of enactment. If this were the case, it would be irrelevant to speak of inadequacies of any kind in the art-thing, even to say that "the artist seems capable only of part of an aesthetic experience." The aesthetic enactment is like pregnancy: there cannot be a "little" of it—it is there or it is not. And, as in pregnancy, the act of conceiving is distinguishable from that of delivery into the open world. It is possible to conceive, but to have difficulty in the delivery. Our analogy breaks down only at one point: in art, the "baby" is fully delivered to and for oneself (which is the only necessary form of its delivery), even before it is delivered in the construction of the public directive record of it. It is foolish and a waste of time to analyze the art-thing in its possible defects without first determining whether or not it really is an art-thing, rather than some other kind of thing. Such identification cannot be made merely by examining technique according to some pre-established model, or some generalization from what techniques have been in other things recognized to be art-things.

Why deliver the aesthetic presence at all in the way of making its public record, if the full and proper delivery of it is nothing else but the enactment? This is a question over which many inquirers have puzzled, and which has lead certain of them to cancel the distinction between the enactment and the record of the enactment.[88] Such cancellation is not so bad when it is made in favor of the living enactment, but, when it amounts to saying that the art-thing is the whole of the art work, it annuls even the art-thing in its important role as concrete public record of aesthetic purposings. Within the context of the account here given, the question practically answers itself. The making of the directive record or the art-thing calls for an entirely different explanation than does the enactment of the aesthetic presence, however much the two are wedded together in the context of aesthetic purposing and in life.

One who makes art-things is impelled to do so from motives which are other than aesthetic: a different posture in purposing is involved. Beethoven might as well have whistled his symphonies silently to himself—he would have been no less the artist. If he chose to set down the special marks which correspond to certain qualities of sounds and their arrangements, it must be because he wanted to be able to remember how the music was to be re-enacted, or to share such enactment with others—for whatever reason. In either case, the possibilities are enormous. He could, for example, very well have wanted simply to "hear" his music once again, that is, to help himself re-enact it. Or he could have wanted to see the evidences around him of being the composer that he and others thought he was or, again, he may have simply had a compulsion to do it, deriving some personal non-aesthetic satisfaction therefrom. If he did it for others, he may have wanted to cause others to admire him, or he may have been impelled by a sense of obligation

---

[88] The distinction between the aesthetic enactment and the record seems not very clearly made by Croce; perhaps his idealistic presuppositions prevent him from doing so.

to share his musical enactments with others, or for any number of
other reasons.

What might be called the most appropriate or authentic reasons
for making the art record for oneself or for others may, from our
point of view, be said to be the following:

When for oneself, the making of the directive record can and
often does help in the enactment itself of the aesthetic presence, as
an operation performed contemporaneously with and for the sake
of the enactment. Rare, indeed, is the person whose power of feeling and imagination is such that his aesthetic formations can clearly
and distinctly become actualized without the more obvious embodiment of overt actions such as are involved in the construction of
the art-thing. Resort to such added activity is almost unavoidable,
considering that we are beings who are in their very constitution
embodied beings, that is, beings the very locus of whose manner
of being is action. And while, of course, action of some sort is always involved in the aesthetic enactment, the native form of it is,
most of the time, much too subtle and elusive for us to help us
hold our enactment steady and in place while it is forming. We
compound the action, therefore, and magnify its power. This is
the sense in which it can be said that, although some bodily action
always corresponds to the enactment of art as its necessary accom-
paniment, most all of us have need for a more overt action in aesthetic purposing. Thus it is that the painter "finds" his colors and
schemes of color while manipulating pigments, and actors and
dancers "find" their characters while they rehearse their parts. Thus
it is, also, that, in trying to "see" the art work hanging on the
museum wall, we sometimes move our arms and hands as if to do
what the painter did in making the art-thing. When the artist has
in fact made a public art-thing contemporaneously with his enactment of the presence, he might very well afterwards choose to
destroy it, or never wish to show it to any other person, which
would indicate the special character of its use. It makes no sense to
speak of "destroying" the enactment itself, for this can only be enacted or not. Only *things* can be destroyed.

In regard to making the art-thing for another, or for other persons, the most generous thing that can be said is that the motive
springs from a man's sense of the social and the moral. The sense
in which we mean it has little or nothing to do with "doing good,"
"obeying the moral law," or being a "good" man according to some
prescription. It has to do, rather, with the existential effort and

decision to be oneself authentically. Existentially and concretely speaking, the real "other" is no intellectual abstraction or generalization, but a part of oneself that one needs in order to be himself.

My choice of myself involves my choosing others to choose me, and to choose me as choosing myself. The more exact formula could be put only in very cumbersome language, such as: The concrete "other person," for me, is whoever enters into my life-world whom I can actually choose as a free chooser who chooses me to be a free chooser of him as a free chooser of me as a chooser of myself. But the formula, so put, still lacks the idea that, in so choosing the "other," I choose him, at the same time, to choose himself as choosing me to choose him as self-chooser. The point here is that existential ethics, of the kind at least that we here contemplate, countenances "being free to be free" as the only moral good, and that pursuit of such good for any man requires others not, indeed, to *do* him good (for, how can this kind of good be "given" or "done" to another?), but to be or to enact themselves as freedom *with* him. In the final analysis, no man can really do anything for any other man except choose him in his very soul to be a free and independent part-agency in his own self-project in his life-world. It would be superfluous to add that, on this basis, being a moral man is the most difficult thing in the world—as difficult, in fact, as being one's self. On this basis, also, the dishonest sentimentality that "the good man loves everybody" must be put aside, for who of the others can or cannot help me be myself is determined by no ready-made rule or precept; I disclose this to myself in the choosing of the other or others in my concrete life-situations. Being good has to do with my own condition of being. At times a man can honestly only choose others who, by every abstract and institutionalized standard, are what are called "bad" men to help him honestly to be himself; just as, under other conditions of his being, he finds his ontological co-makers of himself in persons who are reputed to be "good" in the accepted conventional sense.

That one cannot choose everybody goes without saying, unless we pervert the sense of "choose" and reify the abstraction "everybody." All there is that is genuinely moral about any such statement is the individual intention of him who declares it, if he means it in the form in which the Judeo-Christian Golden Rule is stated. Here, in order to understand the meaning of "neighbor," one ought to go to the story of the Good Samaritan,[89] where it is plainly indicated that

[89] Tillich, *The New Being* (New York: Charles Scribner's Sons, 1955), p. 30.

one's neighbor is not "everybody," but the person who can get the
help he needs from you alone in a concrete existential situation,
and who is the only person in the same situation whom you need in
order to be the kind of person you choose to make of yourself by
your very act.[90] The possibility of any man being able to choose
every other man on earth in this same way is one which, in the
first place, could be ascertained only *ex post facto* (which is physi-
cally impossible), and, secondly, is significant only as the attribute
of a god. The truth of the matter is that we all truly *encounter* in
the real and concrete situations of our existence few persons, let
alone persons whom we can choose as co-makers of our very being.
And, what is even more important, our own condition of being is
rarely such that we are aroused to the need to be our selves, which
alone can make our moral choice of others possible. There is no
intention in what we are saying to discredit general principles and
abstract moral commands for what they concretely are in themselves,
namely, tendentious and hortatory invitations for existing individuals to choose to be and to do according to certain pre-figured
plans of selfhood and of action. If the existing individual can
honestly fit them into the honest project of his self as a freedom,
then, obviously, even these can in some sense or other be called
good.

Interpersonal existential encounter is rare and difficult. Most of
us are fortunate if we find one other person as co-maker of our
self in the sense just explained. Often, too, we invent "true friends"
and "lovers" out of desperation. Often (perhaps always, to some
extent or other) we project our inventions on to the real other
whom we can and do choose and this, as a matter of fact, makes
the collaboration even more mutually creative, since we help one
another to see what else we could be, good or bad, which can help
us mutually to be our self and not be what we disown. In any
event, such is the need which impels us to make outer signs, to
beacon, as it were, in the direction of others. The artist who has
strong propensities in the direction of making art-things is a special
example of such a need for others. An excess of this need may explain, perhaps, the mode of life and behavior of the many artists
who, to the conventional outsider, may appear as dissolute and law-
less in the conduct of their lives. *Eros,* as Plato knew, is the hunger
for self-identifying being for the other.

There are other more or less proper, more or less authentic uses

[90] A. B. Fallico, *The Quest for Authentic Existence,* pp. 88, 94.

to which the art-things which are exhibited everywhere in any society may be put. Despite everything we have said to distinguish art from propaganda, it should be obvious that a thing which is a genuine art-thing, can be also an effective piece of propaganda, calculated to help arouse men to certain actions, to stir their emotions, to get them to buy or to sell, and so on. Such things will be art-things, not because, but in spite of such uses. The propriety or impropriety of the use (which can be judged only on grounds other than aesthetic) rests on expediency and utility but, finally, also on moral grounds. Propaganda, for example, which invites men to choose unfreedom of being is evil, no matter how implemented. And in this category would fall any and all other uses of the art-thing which lend themselves to inhumanity, human self-deception, escape, and self-alienation generally. It is at this point that an activity which in itself is spontaneous, blameless, essentially good, becomes the instrument of an evil will, a will to self-annihilation. The Nazi lampshades made of human skin illustrate perfectly this final misuse of art. If art, then, feeds with new and fresh vision the very life of morality, the moral sense of our humanity takes precedence over its misuse at this point. The final limits of both art and morality are the self-affirmation or self-negation of freedom which makes both art and morality possible.

CHAPTER SIX

The Existential Import

of Art Criticism

ON THE WORD WHICH IS ABOUT THE FIRST WORD

The ways of speaking about speech are many, depending on what kind of doing or purposing activity the speech talked about represents. Our doings are of many kinds. "Speech" which does nothing-and-everything—speech-in-general—is an abstraction. When we speak about such abstraction, we do not speak about speech in the concrete, though in speaking about it, we most certainly do something which only under examination and inspection can be determined in its true character.

If, as we have maintained, art is the first speech or speech itself, what is the speech which purposes to speak about it in the way we denominate "art criticism"? (Except indirectly, in a few necessarily very condensed illustrations, what we have been doing throughout this work is not art criticism.)

Our concrete approach to this question would seem to require the notion of some sort of joint effort, some conjunction of pur-posings which, though cooperating intimately in a single project, nevertheless remain what they are separately and in their own right. The partnership of efforts is plainly indicated by the words "art," and "criticism." And it is interesting to note immediately that the very words speak of radically different, mutually exclusive, kinds of effort. Aesthetic purposing, as we have already seen, does nothing which even remotely resembles criticism; taken separately, criticism makes no aesthetic presences. Yet, in union, they somehow work perfectly together. What is the nature of this joint effort? How is it possible? What does it accomplish?

In approaching these questions, the first and most important thing we must understand is that though the artist, in doing art, has no need to do criticism, the art critic, in doing his art criticism, must be able to enact the aesthetic presentation he wishes to talk about. This is a little more involved than it sounds, for the sense in which the art critic must be artist is twofold: he must be able to speak in the manner of the first utterance which is the art work he wishes to talk about and he must also be able to make his own first speech by which to say what he has to say concerning the work of art he wishes to criticize. The work of art speaks for itself in any case, so that the critic's job is never to speak *for,* but only *about* it, and this is the critic's own first utterance. This can only mean that, successful or unsuccessful (in the sense in which such evaluations apply to the art-thing), the work of criticism is, at the same time, a work of art on its own. If it were not, it could not speak at all or say anything. The idea that the work of criticism must itself be a work of art can be put in more familiar, though less precise ways, such as that the critic "must speak for himself," or that he must "really tell us how he feels," or "be sincere," and so on. Incidentally, what is true of the work of art criticism and the critic in this connection is true also of any project which calls for speech. Even the most obstruse and abstract scientific work must be "expressed," as we say, and the expression of it—the thing-expression corresponding to the art-thing in the work of art—can be successful, partly successful, or unsuccessful, like any art-thing.

From that aspect of the work of art criticism having to do with the work of art as such, and with the critic's own utterance, the work of criticism is a compounded, interpenetrating original speech. But if this were all there was to it, it would be simply another work of art, however complex. Many supposed critical studies of works of art are of this sort. A posture in purposing which is other than the aesthetic one enters into the making of the art-criticism if it is properly such.

So persistent and pervasive has the artist's resentment and suspicion of the art critic been throughout the centuries, that one has come to think of the phenomenon as almost natural and unavoidable. The non-artist—any man, that is, in his non-aesthetic moments

—tends to view this as indicative of the artist's self-centered and idiosyncratic nature. The art critic rarely pays heed to the artist's complaints. But in some instances at least, the traditional feud rests on a very serious issue, for the great majority of those who assume the role of critics are, as is well known, not themselves creators of art objects in the common meaning of the expression. This would not in itself cause any trouble, since appearances do not determine anything, or should not, in the light of this present view of the aesthetic which makes it a common possession of all men. Some of the critics of the critics have had in mind much more than the appearances. They intended to say that art critics, for the most part, attempt either to speak about the work of art without being able to enact the particular work they purport to be discussing, or examine it in its character as art-thing only, or else concern themselves with matters belonging to some non-aesthetic context altogether. The habit of the Marxist critic, for instance, to concentrate on the political uses of the art-thing is well known. Insofar as this is the basis of the artist's complaint, his resentment and criticism of the critic is well taken, and quite an important one at that.

The critic who does not or cannot enact the art work for himself, cannot address himself to it, let alone say anything about it. This does not mean that such a critic therefore must be *doing* nothing, or saying nothing. His saying or speaking may be a work of art all its own, even if it has nothing to do with the work of art he appears to be talking about. His project, extraneous to the task of art criticism under these circumstances, may be one of many. It may be propaganda for certain established or not established moral, aesthetic or other conceptions of human value; or obedience to the policies of a newspaper or publication. It may be the attempt to achieve a reputation as art critic; or a way of telling the artist that he likes or dislikes him. Or it may even be a secret revenge on his mother who might have subjected him, when young, to stand facing the wall before Whistler's *Mother*. The project of the criticism of art criticism is an interesting one.

Ability and disposition to enact the particular art work are prime requisites in art criticism even if, in themselves, these can yield no criticism of art. To determine what there is, which goes beyond the concrete enactment, it is important now to say that the enactment cannot be undertaken by the critic for the purpose of his criticizing it, but simply for its own sake. The reason for saying this, which is as obvious as it may seem puzzling, is that the art work cannot be enacted at all, except as it is enacted simply for its own sake. Aesthetic purposing *makes* its own kind of actuality, and does not implement any other, including that which is resident in the critic's own interests. There must first be something there to see, before there can be anything done with or about it, and the seeing of it must be disinterested, if the genuine article is to appear. The art work is not made as something to be criticized, or awaiting criticism. The criticism is an enterprise all its own, which the critic must not confuse with his enactment of the work of art, no matter how much the former depends on the latter.

But why add criticism to the enactment if the enactment calls for nothing else? The simple fact is that, as in the case of making the art-thing or record, the call for doing something else over and beyond the enactment represents a different kind of interest and activity. In itself, critical activity or purposing makes neither works of art, nor the rules for making works of art. It determines only *if* aesthetic purposing is truly enactable with respect to the apparent art-thing of which it speaks (determines whether the thing is an art-thing or not) and, if it is so, what the import of this enactment is for the total existential condition of man in the vital and concrete situation of the time when the critic actually is speaking. This last statement implies that "time-less" criticism, when it is attempted, is certainly not art criticism (and, incidentally, not easily identifiable as a project). The actuality of art criticism, like that of art itself, is always contemporary, even if the work discussed is Homer's *Iliad* (there is no concrete Homer's *Iliad* except in the present enactment of it).

If the important question be asked: Who is it that assigns such a function to art criticism, and with what justification?, we would not take refuge in convenient and unself-accounting abstractions like "reason," or "common sense," or "all reputable art critics." Only existing men are self-accounting in what they say; they alone are answerable for their assertions. The final justification for the statement can reside nowhere else than in the sincerity with which the existing individual confronts himself, art, and existence. Any man must take his chances here. To me it appears that both existence and art (as well as everything else that is not art) inherently are such in their very being as to call for ever-renewed identification and appraisal in what they mean to, and for, one another. Criticism in this sense, is nothing superimposed upon existence and art, but something to which they themselves give birth for their own mutual improvement—an improvement which is measured, of course, in terms finally of the freedom which they both basically are.

The first of the functions of art criticism mentioned above—namely, the identification, the *spotting* of the aesthetic enactment as such—divides into a dual undertaking: one negative, and the other positive. Art criticism exposes the fraud where fraud, insincerity, and pretense are present, and it confirms the availability of the positive enactment where this effectively is present. Just to say that such and such is or is not art is not what we here have in mind. Nor is it to pile adjectives on one another with reference to the work in question, as so many self-styled critics are inclined to do. It means confirming or disconfirming the claim for the possibility of the enactment (the art-thing itself represents a claim, apart from any other claims that might be made). It is as if it were said that a certain series of operations would result in a certain actual experience, and someone who tried it afterwards made his report on whether or not this really happens. The report must give convincing evidence that the experiment has been a failure or a success. In the case of art criticism, certain details may be left unspoken only because they are tacitly assumed by those who read or hear the report. Thus the art critic need not give us an account of how he took himself to the museum, nor the literary critic assure us that he performed all the operations involved in reading the book. Not for this, however, must it be thought that such operations are not an integral part of the activity of criticism concretely understood.

The essential evidences of having tried the enactment, on the basis of which the critic can then say whether or not such enactment is possible, have all to do with the careful explication of what we have called the elements together with their orderings in the work of art. This involves a careful description of the art-thing, in its parts and as a whole, in the light of the aesthetic presence or enactment which it directs, locates, and records. The critic traces, as it were, on the art-thing the actual progress of the aesthetic enactment.

THE ART CRITIC AS COLLABORATOR
OF THE ARTIST

The art critic is collaborator of the artist in every man, including the one who specializes in the making of aesthetic directive records or art-things. The collaboration is not a co-enactment or a duplication of the enactment, for each man can only do this for himself. The critic acts, rather, as a guide who not only locates the "place" for the enactment, distinguishing it from other "places" where it is supposed to be possible and is not, but also gives the instructions concerning the way the enactment should proceed. In this way alone does the work of criticism reflect the aesthetic enactment as such. It is necessary, therefore, that such a "guiding map" be drawn in light of the actual enactment. Not infrequently do critics of art produce detailed and carefully drawn maps resembling the genuine ones but which really are irrelevant to the work of art being appraised. Often such pseudo-maps once properly served their purpose in criticism of other works, and then are taken as molds into which any art works must be fitted. Even more often, they are particular adaptations of intellectually pre-established conceptions of what the work of art ought to be.

The way by which genuine art criticism leads up to the enactment of the art presence is always cast in the particular manner and style of the critic. There can be no formula or prescription regarding the speech and the order of speech of the critic: such speech is the critic's own art-thing which, in addition to its own aesthetic enactment as such, holds the possibility of serving as guiding map for the reader or the listener. Everything that was said concerning the uses of art applies here too. Any art-thing can be used, even though the aesthetic enactment itself is not for use. The critic intends his own art-thing to be used as a critical evaluation of another art-thing and its corresponding enactment. It is this intention which invests the critic with moral responsibilities in the same way that it does the artist who also makes art-things for his aesthetic enactments. Such moral responsibility centers around the critic's choice and recognition of the artist's free effort in the choice of himself (the critic) as a freedom.

In the critic's construction of his identifying map, the identi-

fication and the mapping constitute a single process which is analogous to the making of the original art presence whose record the
critic examines. The whole and the identification of the whole
emerge with the parts and the identification of the parts. In the
whole, however, the elements are spotted and laid out for inspection.
Each critic does this in his own way, by his own devices, and in his
own language. If the critic is speaking to a present audience about
a painting which stands before him, for example, part of his discrimination of and commentary on the parts (or art-thing-element-
things) might very well involve pointing and other gestures. A less
inhibited critic might very well indicate what he perceives in the
art-thing by the movements and direction of his whole body
together with sounds of one kind or another. If the art-thing is not at
hand, the art critic may use drawn indicators or charts of all kinds,
the literary critic may use quotations or excerpts from the work,
accounts of the plot, and so on. It is significant that almost all
critics will, in one way or another, bring in the name of the creator
of the art piece by saying, "Cézanne here does such and such," or
"Shakespeare here expresses such and such feeling, idea, or action."
And, as for the elements, so also for their organic composition in
the whole and among the parts. But whatever the critic's own
choice and preference of means for doing all this, his discriminative
and relating efforts amount always to an original utterance of his
own, wedded to action calculated to guide the listener or reader to
enact felt-images according to a certain order and plan. When the
listeners and readers are aesthetically perceptive, the work of the
critic can be greatly condensed. Sometimes the truly great critic
can open up the world of the art work for a listener or reader with
a single sentence. The language of criticism lends itself peculiarly
to interchangeable references: "chiaroscuro," which usually refers
to certain qualities of a painting, can very well help reveal something about a piece of music, and the same can be said of "color,"
"movement," "dissonance," "harmonious," and so on.

But it would be altogether too narrow and inaccurate a view of
the critic's work if we limited it merely to the identification and
mapping of the art-thing. For although it is true that some critics
choose and prefer to do no more than this—and are no less helpful
for it—there are others who can and do go beyond. These we
should perhaps call the greater critics. Their collaboration is not
only with the artist in every man, but with the existing man taken

in the fullness of his being—the whole man—insofar as he is awakened to the need for self-knowledge and self-being.

THE ART CRITIC AS COLLABORATOR
OF THE PHILOSOPHER

Art criticism finds its larger and more comprehensive scope when, in addition to identifying and mapping the progress of the aesthetic enactment on the art-thing, it also attempts to "read" or to interpret its import for the existential condition of man. The assignment of this task to the art critic is consistent with all we have been saying about art and about human existence. The work of aesthetic purposing everywhere speaks for the human condition— the despair, the hope, the joy of existence. Art criticism would be less than the serious undertaking which it is in its higher reach, if it did not concern itself with the existential import of art.

In view of this larger scope, it would be superfluous to say that the art critic is collaborator of the philosopher in every man, including one who writes down and publishes his philosophizings, were it not for the fact that "philosophy" and "philosophizing" are all things to all men. We make an issue of it here only because we consider philosophy or philosophizing to be that particular posture in purposive activity wherein self-consciousness of purposing—no matter what or how it is purposing—is achieved. Art, being essentially freed, as well as free purposing or spontaneity, forming its possible self-in-its-life-world, must have a special and unique relationship to the philosophical endeavor. But equally important is the fact that even in this more comprehensive and deeper reach, art criticism as such is not the same as the philosophical effort, it can only collaborate with the progress and formation of philosophical thought. In this respect, in fact, the relation between philosophy and the aesthetic enactment is more direct and constitutive than that between philosophy and art criticism. Art criticism is intermediate.

This, too, should now be evident. For philosophy, like art criticism or anything else which requires speech in order to manifest itself even to him who makes it, can find its original word only in the aesthetic enactment. If it appears sometimes that the philosopher is in no sense a poet, this is because of what we consider grave and harmful misconceptions regarding both art and philosophy. Lest any reader imagine that we wish to discredit such great philosophers as Kant, or Hegel, or Dewey (notoriously unclear and exasperating writers), we hasten to say that a man may be a great philosopher yet a poor writer or speaker, just as he may be an artist with little ability to construct the record of his aesthetic enactments. There are truly fine technicians in the family of artists who paint clearly and with great dexterity but who, despite this, are not artists at all according to the views herein put forth. And there are philosophers who write and think clearly and systematically, but who are far from doing what we here call philosophy. It is even possible to speak and to think clearly about nothing at all. One need only open some of our scholarly philosophical journals, or visit any suburban art exhibit to see these things done.

Insofar as the art critic helps to open up the actuality of the work of art, he not only helps the artist in the philosopher to make language as such (which is always aesthetic in its concrete character, and which the man—not just the artist in the philosopher—needs for his essential humanity), but helps both artist and philosopher to envision the freely actualized possibilities of being which are the aesthetic presences themselves. The question of how can such envisionments help the philosopher in his philosophizing we leave for the *Note* which concludes this book. Aesthetic presences constitute the only models or archetypes for possible actualities of concrete being. It is, of course, true that they are only models of possible actualities, but unless the very possibility of such being can be concretely envisioned, there can be no actual and concrete grasp of the existential realities with which the work of the philosopher is concerned. We refer here not merely to the purely logical priority of the possible to the actual, but to the very structure of the concrete.

The collaboration between art criticism and philosophy is such that though the philosopher need not be an art critic in the proper sense, the art critic must be something of a philosopher. This follows from the fact that, at least in its larger scope, art criticism must reach into the world of the art work to exhibit, shall we say, its existential flavor. A critical study of the *Divine Comedy* would certainly be incomplete without some examination of its view of man and of freedom, albeit as aesthetic possibility only, just as a critical study of Picasso's *Guernica* would be incomplete without serious attention to the debacle of modern man seen through peculiarly Spanish sensitivities and the revolutionary situation.

Concerning this deeper, wider identification and mapping of the art-thing which the art critic may make, it must be said that, although always in the unique form of the particular work of art, the fundamental existential themes exhibited are, in any case, just a few: life, death, love, hope, and desperation. The variations on these basic themes are of course countless. Few, also, are the final positions that existing man can take on human existence and its concrete situations: *yea! nay! perhaps,* and *who cares?* Here, too, the possible variations make the number of positions seem endless. In the work of art, and hence too in the work of the critic, both the themes and the human existential attitudes on life do not come in the form of intellectual demonstration or philosophical disclosures.

Finally, it is not merely what we know as "philosophical" works of art which lend themselves to the deeper and wider criticism, but any and all works of art. A genuinely philosophical work of art is not one work but two—living, as it were, together. Many of Plato's *Dialogues,* Lucretius' *De Rerum Natura,* and Nietzsche's *Zarathustra,* for example, are of this sort. One can deal with either the philosophy in these works, or the art, or both together—provided one does not confuse the different kinds of purposing involved. It is such confusion of distinguishable efforts which accounts for much of the nonsense written, for instance, about Plato's famous Myths. The philosophical or existential import which is inherent in and indistinguishable from the aesthetic enactment is not the work of philosophical purpose as such, and hence not philosophy in its own right. It is, rather, that same possible reality of the art presence when it is viewed in its bearing on existence. Such a view of the art presence can be taken with any and all works of art, even the most geometrical Mondrian. A single line, provided it intends an aesthetic felt-image, can in fact contain the most complete commentary on human existence.[91]

[91] This is particularly true of much classical Chinese and Japanese painting where the whole work often consists of a few brush-strokes. Oriental poetry, often consisting of but a few words or lines, is another illustration.

A Note on Art & Philosophy

Like life itself whose self-conscious inspection it is, philosophy ends where it begins, and begins where it ends: our concluding remarks take us back to the beginning.

Purposive activity is many-faceted; philosophy, in which it finds its self-discernment and discriminations, is also many-faceted. For though philosophy is only one among the facets of the human existent, there is no facet which cannot enter into the focus of its inspection. Thus an aesthetics or philosophy of art must be part of a self-accounting.

That such self-accounting is in every case the account of him who makes it, there can be no doubt. Philosophy is like art in this respect. But if this were all, its essential worth would be only aesthetic. And while this would be worth enough, it could never justify philosophy's claim to truth, in addition to the truthfulness which it must possess in any case. The account of art and language attempted in these pages at least indicates how it might be possible to explain the undeniable fact that—despite our irremediable loneness of being as existing individuals—we *do* speak with one another and, in so doing, join our very beings in a common, concrete utterance.

That old bugaboo of philosophy known as *solipsism* consists of an accusation often levelled by one philosopher against another's position, that the accused philosopher's consciousness is, in the theory he is expounding, the whole of reality, and that the external world (including other persons) is merely a representation of that consciousness, having no independent existence. In a way, it is regrettable that solipsism has nearly always been used as accusation and rarely, if ever, for the important existential element of truth it contains. For solipsism stands ever as an indispensable caution that the independent ontological status of the *other,* whether thing or person, is no easily ascertainable matter; and it establishes the exact basis of moral responsibility. The existential being does not escape his loneness merely by constructing or entertaining theories, but by becoming committed to the *other's* existence, disclosing it to himself in his first speech: a man must will and feel that the world and other men *be,* because he wills himself to be. In the cosmic venture of being, the beings who really encounter and who associate with one another must each find the other in himself, as himself. Their togetherness is not conveniently prearranged to make that moral and aesthetic effort superfluous.

But how is it possible for us to speak what is true—in the case of aesthetics, what is true about art? The two questions—what is philosophical truth, and what is philosophical truth about art—are inseparable, and their consideration would require many volumes. We can here only give a last look at what we have already done, in order to help the reader better locate our present effort in the ocean (or should we say desert?) of claims regarding what is and what is not philosophical truth and how this truth relates to the truthfulness that is art.

One sense of "truth," we have already alluded to; truth, namely, in the sense of objective and therefore necessarily abstract truth. This need not concern us here since, as we hope, we have made it clear that philosophy is a quest after concreteness: objective truth is not, as such, self-accounting (which is what justifies, and calls for, a philosophy of science).

Philosophy is the quest after concreteness, and philosophy of art is the quest after the concreteness of art; but philosophy is also a concrete quest after concreteness. The emphasis is to indicate not only that it is the concrete fact that philosophy studies, but that it engages the existent with the whole of his being, shunning the safe "distance" of mere objectivity.

Now, to be fully engaged with one's whole being in the effort to understand art or anything else, is to be engaged affectively, volitionally, and cognitively all in one, and to know or realize it. This is not to propose some novel theory about human knowledge, but simply to describe an actual phenomenon which, though rarely dignified by the title of philosophy, must nevertheless be all the philosophy there is in any philosophy. Professor Bowsma once pointed out that Socrates was obeying his oracle, and that all the rest of what he said was detail. "Obeying one's oracle" involves a great deal, including knowing that one is obeying his oracle, and the details and accompaniments are important too. In this context, "obeying one's oracle" means feeling, acting, and knowing with self-concern in the Kierkegaardian sense; it means obeying one's self in one's innermost existential being. And if the question be asked, For what purpose? the answer can only be: to be the freedom that one is. But, again, this involves much more than appears on the surface.

Though we are freedom itself, the freedom that we are is not gratuitous, assured, or settled in its meaning for us. There is an ancient and enduring quest for the meaning of being whose place has always been usurped by other extraneous interests. Martin Heidegger rightly points out that this quest is not what philosophers know as metaphysics, and we would add that much that is called religion has little to do with this quest. The ancient Hindus revealed a profound grasp of the nature of this quest when they reserved the last portion of a man's earthly existence for the search after his Self. After the age of forty, a man was to drop all his world-roles, including his very name, and retire to the forest to find who or what he is in the ultimate sense. We would say that—not at forty, but at any time of his maturity, not in forests, but in the course of everyday social living—this is a man's most important and all-engaging undertaking. It is, in fact, the final and complete form of the quest after freedom which is life itself.

If philosophy is not the whole of this quest then it must surely be some part of it, some stage of its perhaps endless course. But it would neither be concrete nor of the concrete if, even as the most primitive of stages in the quest, philosophy did not catch some glimpse of the overall meaning of existence. Whatever the final meaning of being may be, it seems certain that—for existing men, in any case—it either is something or some whole state into which they can enter wholly and with their whole being (as they enter into the act of loving when it is real) or it is nothing at all. On this alone, the demand for concreteness in philosophy is justified.

We said that concreteness applies to philosophy in two ways: in what it refers to and in how it refers to it. It speaks of concrete realities, and it is the whole or concrete man who speaks about the concrete realities in the awareness of doing so. But this immediately breaks down into sub-notations, one of which requires only thinking back about what has already been said concerning art and language to be understood. Whether the philosopher speaks of or about anything or not, he cannot but speak; and this can be only in and through his own aesthetic enactments. No more need be said except that a philosopher lacking in (aesthetic) feeling and imagination cannot speak, let alone speak about anything. (This ability is of course distinguished from that involved in making the directive records of concrete speech. The philosopher can be deficient or able on both counts, and in different degrees.)

But another and all-important sub-notation remains, having to do with how the basic and original word of the philosopher comes to acquire the value *truth*. And the first thing to be said is that all language, including the language of the philosopher, is that same first utterance which is the enactment of aesthetic possibility. In the hands of the artist, the full and complete linguistic act is for its own sake only. In the hands of the philosopher, it is something more. The possibility of being-self-in-its-world-together-with-other-selves which constitutes the aesthetic word is, in philosophy, somehow *proposed* as the possibility which is becoming actualized as life-in-the-world. It is as if the philosopher had discovered that a certain aesthetic model for self-in-its-life-world applied to this world. A useful, though somewhat risky analogy for this remarkable "application" might be the apparent connection between pure mathematics and empirical science. Mathematical objects and systems are concededly "ideal" or logical pure possibilities which, like the possibilities of the aesthetic, can be invested with a kind of actuality of their own. We know now that any number of such objects and systems can be constructed, the only limit being the creative mathematician's special kind of imagination. But we know also that not all such systems seem to apply to the real world in the way, say, that Euclidean and non-Euclidean geometries apply to physical and astronomical phenomena. Where there is such a coincidence, it is—as in mathematical physics and the like—almost impossible to tell where the ideal component begins and the physical one ends.

Every philosophical formation proposes some aesthetic possibility as disclosing of being itself to the existent. In this too may be seen the fundamental place and role of what we have called aesthetic sincerity. (Pseudo-philosophies are basically insincere philosophies, or philosophies which are not really convincing, even to him who makes and proposes them.) If you reach far enough into any philosophical proposal, you will find some nucleus of aesthetic intimations. A history of philosophy which sought for these nuclei of insight would be a fascinating project, to say the least.

But what does "to propose" mean in the context in which we are now speaking? On the clarification of this hinges our under-standing of how the truthfulness of art converts into philosophical truth. It is not the aesthetic envisionment as such which converts itself into such truth, but the existing man who does it. In itself, art never proposes anything.

The act of proposal is a practical act—an action. But it is not an action like lifting a chair or chopping down a tree; it is no ordinary project. For although it is not—like art—a purposing without a purpose, philosophical proposal resembles it in that the purpose which it purposes is not prearranged. In this respect, philo-sophy is a search for meaning by an effort which is free even from *having to find any meanings at all.* The philosophical effort is so constituted that it stays free even to assert that the only meaning of being is to have no meaning.

Finally, the proposals of the philosophical endeavor are—before anything else—made by the whole man, to and for himself, out of profound ontological self-concern. A man enters with his whole life into such proposals. If he chooses to share them with others, it is because no man can choose to be free without choosing also his fellow choosers, human and divine.

Index

A

Abstract art, 128

Absurd, the, 47

Action, 61-2, 67, 79, 95, 117, 130-1, 138-9, 144, 150, 153, 168

Actuality, 81, 85, 87, 89, 91, 110, 118, 125, 127, 129, 136, 146-7

Aesthetic, the, 52, 83

Aesthetic:
awareness, 18
completion, 66, 68
ingenuousness, 32
necessity, 29
order, 25-8
possibility, 61
presence, 21, 38, 70, 80-1, 87, 89-90, 124, 144, 147-50, 155, 158-60, 162-3
prophecy, 115
purpose, 42
purposing, 121
renewal, 21, 39
sincerity, 20
spontaneity, 63, 76, 83, 87, 89, 125, 131
transformation of life, 82-3, 85
unity, 29
untruthfulness, 88

Aestheticism, 83

Aesthetics, 56, 119, 164
existential, 8

Agent, 125

Alternation, 47, 49

Apollo, 54

Apollonian, 54-5

Aquinas, St. Thomas, 2, 13, 25

Aristotle, 9, 24, 80, 96

Art, 52, 65, 80, 87, 119-20, 124, 167

Art construct, 40, 41

Art critic, 155-6, 159, 162-3

Art criticism, 154, 156, 158-9, 161
actuality of, 157

Artist, 107-8, 127, 148, 152, 155, 167

Art-object, 18, 21, 23-32, 35, 38, 43, 46, 60

Art presence, 22, 24, 60

Art-*thing*, 107, 137, 143-50, 153, 155-60, 163

Augustine, St., 5

Automatism, 129

Awareness, aesthetic, 18

B

Baldwin, J. M., 75

Beatrice, 81

Beautiful, the, 69-70

Beethoven, 23, 30, 102, 120, 149

Being, 53, 58, 60, 70, 72-4, 77, 79, 85, 95, 109, 112, 165, 167
meaning of, 166
possible, 20, 22

Being-in-the-world, 4

Being-self-in-a-world, 47

Being-there, 6, 44

Bird in Flight, 139-40, 143, 147

Body, 68, 137-39, 141, 143-4, 150

Boehme, J., 9

Botticelli, 81

Bowsma, O., 101, 165

Brahman, 113

Brancusi, 138, 140-1, 143-7

Braque, 81